Blessings
Mike Piazza

Prophetic Renewal

Also by Rev. Piazza

Gay by God:
How to be Lesbian or Gay and Christian

The Real antiChrist:
How America Sold Its Soul

Queeries:
Questions Lesbians and Gays Have for God, second edition

Prophetic Renewal

Hope for the Liberal Church

Rev. Michael S. Piazza

Sources of Hope Publishing
Dallas, Texas 75235

PROPHETIC RENEWAL: Hope for the liberal church.
Published by Sources of Hope Publishing
P.O. Box 35466
5910 Cedar Springs Road
Dallas, TX 75235
800-501-4673

ISBN 978-1-887129-12-1

Printed in the United States

Cover design by David Montejano
Back cover photo by Shawn Northcutt

This book is dedicated to church leaders who refused to choose between their heads and their hearts but gave both to the Spirit. I am blessed to share this journey with many such women and men at the Cathedral of Hope.

Table of Contents

Introduction
Growth or Death?

When a new church reaches an average attendance of around 115-120 adults it can usually afford to support a full-time pastor, and church-planters feel some confidence about its viability. Currently, the largest mainline denomination in the United States loses the equivalent of one viable church each day. The United Methodist Church's membership decline of 71,518 members in 2004 equates to losing approximately 196 members every single day of the year—a church a day. ("United Methodist Church Reports Another Membership Loss," *Associated Press*, July 21, 2005)

Now, before going too far, I should confess that I am personally responsible for some of that loss. After leading several United Methodist churches through seasons of growth, the Methodist Church decided I was not the kind of pastor they wanted, hence there was one less United Methodist in the world.

It was one of the most painful experiences I have had. The denomination I had been a part of almost all of my life—where I had learned to read the Bible, been baptized, confirmed and ordained—decided that I didn't belong there. Ultimately, I have concluded that they were correct; I did NOT belong. My vision of the church of Jesus Christ is that it is the best thing that has ever happened to the human race, at least since Jesus' departure. As a result, there is absolutely no reason that it should be dying. I don't belong in a church or denomination that has missed the value of the gift that is theirs.

Every time I recall the rejection of the Methodist bureaucrats, I think of the words of Joseph to his brothers: "You meant it for evil, but God meant it for good." (Genesis 50:20) So it has been in my life. Since leaving the United Methodist church, I have become pastor of one of the largest and fastest growing churches in America. In fact, the church I led for almost 20 years grew to be larger than any United Methodist church in the conference of which I was a member. They might have meant to exclude me from ministry, but, obviously, God had other plans.

Over the past two decades, it has been my privilege to be the pastoral leader of the Cathedral of Hope, as it grew from 280 members to almost 4,000. The consolidated budget grew from $280,000 to more than $4 million. All of this happened despite the congregation burying almost 1,500 young men who died of AIDS. We built a liberal congregation in one of the most conservative cities in America. The only reason I dare to write this book is that if it can happen here and under these circumstances it can happen anywhere.

My hope is that the insights that follow will be of help to you as, together, we seek to restore the Church of Jesus Christ to vibrancy and growth. We simply cannot allow Christianity to become a fundamentalist, vindictive, excluding religion. I believe our progressive values and vision are most congruent with the Gospels' witness of who Jesus was and what he taught. We cannot allow the world to come to believe Jesus is the vengeful fundamentalist messiah that, all too often, he is depicted to be. We have a word of grace to speak to the soul of a hurting world. We cannot be silent. We must not allow our witness to die away at the rate of one congregation each day. It is my conviction that what we have to offer is exactly what people need at this time in history. We must not be apologetic or timid in offering it.

After several requests from colleagues in progressive and liberal churches, I decided to try to identify and record what we learned about growing a vibrant and vital church in a most challenging place. As my dear friend and mentor Dr. Lyle Schaller always teaches, I began by making a list. There was a long list of principles, which might be helpful. However, I have discovered with my own church family that I usually lose my audience when I get to the lists of the Bible. Like me, though, they always love the stories. So, since I lack Lyle's great aptitude for making lists interesting, I thought it best to stick with what I do well. Another mentor, Dr. Fred Craddock, taught me to be a storyteller. My congregation owes him a great debt, though they might have gotten more sleep if my preaching had been shaped by a different homiletics professor.

What follows is the story of one church. It is told from the perspective of one pastor. My hope is that you will read it as a parable. The point, in case I fail to make it, is that if we can do it you can too; or, more to the point, if I can do it you certainly can too. My prayer is that this story may inspire insights in you. As Fred is fond of saying, "Good preaching is not so much speaking *to* people as it is speaking *for* them." If you hear your own story in this then it has been a success. If you gain insights into your story then it has been blessed. If it prompts in you ideas for renewing your church then my prayers have all been answered.

Let me begin with a bit of a disclaimer. In the South a critical skill for a pastoral survival is eating fried chicken. The third week of June in 1973 I ate fried chicken on six consecutive days. That was my first week as a student pastor of a small circuit of Methodist churches in South Georgia. Today, in middle age, I seldom eat anything that has been fried. Still, that skill I learned as a young pastor stands me in good stead when I pick up books like the one in your hand. You see, when you eat fried chicken you eat the meat and leave the bones. So, too, as you read what follows, take what nourishes you and leave the rest. My only caution comes from my personal encounters with scripture: often that which offends is ultimately that which has the most to say.

Our churches will either grow or die. That is how it is with you and me as well. What we have to offer is too valuable to allow it to die. What do you have to lose? In the most difficult of circumstances, the most unlikely person (me) resurrected a church and participated in a miracle. As I have said before, if it can happen to me it can happen to you. So, let the adventure begin!

Blessings,
Michael

Chapter 1
Let Us Begin With Grace

The majority of pastors and church leaders today are part of a generation of women and men who grew up in the church. Most of us grew up in churches of the denomination in which we now serve. Church is the very air we breathe. We are no more objective about it than a fish could be about the water in which it swims. Yet, we differ from those fish because we have the capacity to make changes that can greatly impact the reality in which we live.

Perhaps like you, I fell in love with the church when I was just a child. My parents were not particularly church-going folk. They held no antipathy toward the church, but the two of them came from vastly different backgrounds. My father is the son of Roman Catholic Italian immigrants. Protestants were as foreign to them as everything else American that existed outside the suburban Chicago Italian neighborhood in which he was raised. He was not alone in this reality, and the current rate of Hispanic migration makes this history very relevant to the future of mainline Protestant churches in America. We must begin by gaining an appreciation for the perceptions of those migrating from countries where "church" is synonymous with Roman Catholicism. This is a lesson we did not learn well the first time and that, in part, accounts for our declining membership while Catholicism is experiencing continued and explosive growth.

My mother was a nominal Protestant. She grew up in the rural South, in a community where there was not a Roman Catholic Church within an hour's drive. In her hometown, First Baptist Church stood on one corner and was just slightly larger and slightly less affluent than the First Methodist Church, which stood on the opposing corner. Somewhere in town there probably was a small Presbyterian, Lutheran, Pentecostal or Episcopal Church. In one section of town there were several exclusively African-American churches, which remain largely segregated even to this day. Like so many, her family went to church for special occasions or in times of crisis. Since her parents also didn't grow up going to church, her family had no sense of loss or its absence from their lives.

When church is where you "live and breathe and have your being," such attitudes are beyond our comprehension. Yet, increasingly, we are faced with the challenge of speaking to a completely "unchurched" generation. If we cannot tell them why we are relevant to their daily lives we may as well start a going-out-of-business sale.

Fortunately for me, one of the things the mainline church has always done well is children's ministry. One summer, when I was about eight-years-old, I went to Vacation Bible School at the neighborhood Methodist church. There, devoted teachers and an old semi-retired preacher named Simon Peter Clarey loved me into loving Jesus and Jesus' church. That day, I went to church and never left, though there have been a couple of close calls.

Looking back, I realize that I was already keenly aware that there was something queer about me. I didn't like to do many of the things that other boys my age enjoyed. The gentleness and tenderness that adults found so endearing in a little boy made him the target of teasing and ridicule by other boys. While I managed to avoid most of the abuse so many of my gay and lesbian friends endured, there was a major secret I always carried around on the inside. Back then, I had no words for it, and it would be more than a decade before I did, but still it was there. It well may have been this unnamed angst that made my heart fertile soil for seeds of grace. This internal secret, that even I didn't yet know, gave me a very clear feeling that rejection was the inevitable consequence of disclosure.

Then I found a safe place. There, for the first time in my young life, I found a place where people accepted me and loved me, even though I wasn't related to them. Here, they taught me that God knew everything about me and loved me still. That was what they said grace was. It was clear to me that they believed that God loved me regardless of secrets yet unknown. There was something so powerful and authentic about their witness that I accepted it on such a deep level that nothing has ever been able to take it from me.

Unfortunately, 16 years later, that same denomination told me that the people at that little church where I had been baptized and confirmed were wrong about grace and unconditional welcome. "Oh, everyone is welcome ... except you and your kind" was their message. While that rejection caused an emotional and vocational crisis for me, it did not create a spiritual crisis for me. Fortunately, my soul chose to believe the witness of those Sunday School teachers and that retired Methodist preacher, rather than the current fear-based way my Mother Church rejects, or provisionally tolerates, its lesbian and gay children.

The church I fell in love with welcomed a little boy who was different, whose parents weren't even part of that church, and who had nothing more than his weekly quarter to give. It is my opinion that there is a world of hurting people, straight and gay, who are looking for, and longing for, just such a church today. While it may be lesbian, gay, bisexual and transgender people who are labeled by many denominations and congregations as "unfit" for full membership or ordination, the message is clearly felt by every queer-feeling person. Every honest unchurched person in America fears, at least on a subconscious level, that if a local pastor or congregation knew their secrets they would be humiliated and rejected. Even those churches who believe that "God is still speaking" and seek to be unconditionally welcoming, have a great deal of hurt to heal before they have much credibility.

Having fallen in love with the church as a little boy, I spent the next eight years harassing my parents to take me to church every time the doors were opened. When we moved from one small town to another, I had to seek out my own church home. I decided to begin with the Methodist church since that was where I had been baptized and confirmed several years before. The first church I visited was the First United Methodist Church of Statesboro, Georgia. I never visited another.

While I am embarrassed now to admit it, what hooked me on First Methodist was its building. Although this sounds too gay even for me, it was the most beautiful building I had ever seen. The stained glass kept me enchanted through many a sermon that was irrelevant or over my head. It was a gothic building that inspired such awe that I went every Sunday, certain that, if God lived anywhere in Statesboro, this would be "His" house. Going to church with that expectation, I was seldom disappointed.

Through my teenage years I became very involved with church. It was an era when the Methodist Church mandated youth members of committees and the Board. I was able to do it all, even becoming a youth delegate to the governing bodies of the denomination. I came to love the pastor's wife, who talked to me more like a friend than a child. Though she was older than my mother, and I was, by then, a senior in high school, she was one of the first adults to actually take me seriously. One Sunday I attended church alone, as usual. That particular day, I happened to sit next to her during the service. As the sermon came to an end, her husband took off his glasses and looked down at us from that high, gothic pulpit and announced that they were going to be leaving our church.

Like everyone in that room I was shocked. This was very uncommon in Methodist churches, because moving day was in June, and that was still nine months away. I looked up at my friend as she sat there looking appropriately supportive, but I noticed the tears and I also began to cry. After the benediction, she tried to say something to comfort me, and I blurted out, "But if you leave who will teach me how to preach?"

The words were as much of a surprise to me as they were to her. I didn't know that was what I was going to do with my life, at least not consciously. As a lifelong introvert, it didn't seem to be a particularly wise vocational choice. However, a week or so later, she and the pastor invited me over for dinner. After dessert, we sat at the table, and he took a yellow legal pad and outlined for me what the process would be in order for me to become a United Methodist minister. Seven years of college and seminary seemed like a lifetime, but that yellow paper became the governing document for most of the next decade of my life.

I couldn't imagine waiting that long to begin doing ministry, though, so, when I graduated from high school, I took a job as a junior high youth director in my home church. I preached occasionally and taught adult classes. Then, the next year, there was a severe shortage of pastors in the South Georgia Conference. As a result, the district superintendent asked if I would be willing to be the student pastor of a circuit of three very small rural churches. I was terrified, but he assured me that these churches had been around for almost 200 years and there was nothing I could do to kill them. It was the first time a United Methodist denominational leader underestimated me, because I nearly proved him wrong.

Actually, it was a completely wonderful experience. What a perfect place for a young person to learn how to pastor. One church had only 20 members, and I had to assist most of them up the steps into the building each Sunday. All of them were older than my grandparents at that time. What a terrible pastor I must have been, but they never let on. These people were cut of the same cloth as those at that little church where I was baptized and confirmed just a decade before.

Not surprisingly, it was the women of these three little country churches who gave me all the love and encouragement I needed to learn and grow. One week, after I watched "The Autobiography of Miss Jane Pittman," I preached a naïvely rip-roaring sermon about racial justice. Remember this was 1973 in rural South Georgia. In the larger of the three churches—the one that paid most of my salary—there was quite a stir.

That night, when we gathered for a potluck supper, I noticed that most of the men were standing around outside while the women and children were all inside. Suddenly, I looked around the little fellowship hall and it was only me and the kids. The women were crammed into the little kitchen whispering, and the men were still outside talking in low tones. Although no one had said anything to me, I assumed it all had to do with the morning's sermon. Soon, I saw all the women of the church start taking off their aprons, and the kids and I watched as they marched themselves outside. Although I never knew exactly what happened, in a few minutes, everyone, both men and women, returned to the fellowship hall. I noticed almost immediately that the men were all looking a bit chagrined, and they all made it a point to come over and speak to me or clap me on the back.

During the two years I was their pastor, this little church managed to grow enough to eventually leave the circuit and call their own pastor. Several years later, I was invited back to that church to preach a revival, and, after the service, one of the older men said to their new pastor that I was the person who caused the only fight that he and his wife had ever had in 50 years of marriage. "What was the fight about?" my colleague asked innocently. "A sermon," was all the old farmer said. "And who won the fight?" their new pastor asked. "Well, preacher, let's just say that what Brother Mike didn't teach me about race relations in the morning, my wife taught me that night."

That night, I learned that prophets need friends, and the prophetic ministry of the pastor is best done in the context of relationships. All too many mainline pastors let the fear of conflict make them timid, but I am convinced that is the wrong response to the Spirit. We must build relationships with our parishioners that make speaking challenging words a requisite act of integrity. Although our congregations may not agree with us, they will hold us in greater esteem if we speak to them with courage and conviction. We must exchange their affection for their respect in many instances. After a recent sermon against the evil of state-sponsored executions, a member of my congregation reminded me that I was in Texas where capital punishment is a sacrament. While we strongly disagreed, he did shake my hand and say, "I'm glad my pastor calls me to a higher set of values, even when I don't agree."

For eight years, I was a United Methodist student pastor of churches in rural South Georgia. Each of the churches I served grew, some significantly. At the end of my seminary education, though, I finally acknowledged that, as a gay man, something had to change. When I had been ordained, the man who knelt beside me was much older than the rest of us. He had killed a man when he was young, but, in prison, he had become a Christian. Decades later, after being released, he decided to become a Methodist preacher.

Although I had been very successful as a student pastor and received awards and acclaim, I knew that honesty would not be tolerated. While the Bishop gladly and knowingly ordained the convicted killer kneeling beside me, if he had known the truth about me, his hands never would have touched my head.

When I finally came out, the rejection was as utterly complete as I had anticipated. Nothing I had done mattered. All that mattered was that the person I loved was the same gender. About this there was absolutely no grace. I was one of the fortunate ones, though. In anticipation of this day, I had created a wonderful support network, and I left the United Methodist church one Sunday and joined the staff of the mostly gay Metropolitan Community Church the next. That was 1980. Later that year, I also married the man who is still my partner, and we remain in ministry together.

In 1987, we came to Dallas, Texas to become the pastor of the mostly lesbian and gay Metropolitan Community Church of Dallas. It is the story of that church's growth that I'd like to tell you now.

Chapter 2

A Parable of Grace and Resurrection

The General Conference of the Metropolitan Community Church (MCC) was held in Miami, Florida in July of 1987. (Conference planners probably got a really good discount on hotel rooms.) Although I was pastoring a church in Jacksonville, Florida at the time, as I left for that conference, a friend said I was crazy to go to Miami in July. She may have been right. As I sat in the opening business session, two delegates in the row in front of me were talking about the Dallas church. According to them, that church was in real trouble. What was once one of the denomination's strongest congregations was on the verge of collapse, and they concluded that "anyone who went to be the pastor of that church would have to be crazy." They didn't know me, and they had no way of knowing that I had been contacted by the Dallas church about coming to be their next pastor.

The Dallas MCC wrote to me in Jacksonville where I had been the pastor for about four years. Coming from a United Methodist background, moving every four years was the norm for me. Still, I was pretty happy in Jacksonville, and that church had come a long way. They had been firebombed about six months before I came there, and then the pastor had died rather suddenly. At the time, they simply said it was cancer. Later, we learned he probably had AIDS, but, in the early 1980s, none of us knew much about that disease. By the time I got to Jacksonville in 1983, there were only about 30 members left. After I arrived, the church was firebombed again—twice. Four years later, our attendance was close to

300, we had bought property, and we were about to build a new facility. The Miami General Conference gave the Jacksonville church an award for its courage and ultimate resurrection. It was a little church that refused to let hate and fear kill it.

Leaving them would be hard. My partner, Bill, and I owned a business there, and we had built a good life. We were close to my biological family in South Georgia, but not too close. The Dallas church had contacted me twice, and both times I told them how flattered I was, but declined. When they wrote the third time, it was actually Bill who said, "You know, maybe it isn't that God wants us to go to Dallas, but maybe God has someone better in mind for Jacksonville." I told him that not only was that bad theology, but it was not very supportive. He simply grinned and said, "I know."

So, the third time when I wrote back, I told them that if they had not found a pastor by General Conference I would be willing to talk to them. The search committee had already talked to two friends of mine who pastored nearby churches in Florida. Both of them had very negative reactions, so I wasn't very optimistic. Still, I completed their rather extensive questionnaire, and, since I really didn't really want the job, I gave brutally frank answers. I had no idea that they would provide copies of my answers to the whole congregation.

To make a long story shorter, on All Saints Sunday 1987, I stood in the pulpit in Dallas and said, "Good morning. My name is Mike Piazza and apparently I'm your new pastor." It didn't feel quite real. Neither Bill nor I liked Dallas as a city (and all these years later little has changed about that). Mostly, we said yes because we sensed that the church needed a turn-around much like the Jacksonville church had four years before. Fortunately, we had no idea how right we were, or we never would have said yes.

The late 1980s were not a good time in Texas. Dallas was the epicenter of the savings-and-loan crisis that rocked the nation and nearly destroyed the economy. Real estate prices had plummeted. The condominium that the church owned as a parsonage had dropped in value from $135,000 to about $29,000, and, even at that price, there was no market to sell it. The neighborhood where the church was located was in a state of severe decline because of the real estate crash. The crime rate had soared, and it was unsafe to go into the church parking lot alone after dark.

As a result of the recession, the church had laid off most of its staff, and I was asked to take a 25 percent cut in pay to come to Dallas. The building, which was never beautiful when it was new, was in severe disrepair. Roof leaks had left the ceiling and walls stained, and the tile on the floor was cracked and loose. Inadequate in the best of times, now, it was not only too small, but very unattractive. Since several of the largest donors had filed bankruptcy, it was impossible for the church to pay its bills, let alone restore the building.

The annual budget was $280,000, but offerings were not close to that amount. There was $27,000 worth of unpaid bills that the treasurer brought to my office during my first week, asking which ones he should pay. To complicate things further, there were two balloon notes due on the facility. The first was due the first week I arrived, and the other due exactly one year later. Both were in the neighborhood of $80,000, but the church had absolutely no money to pay either. Fortunately, I was able to renegotiate the first one, but the second was held by the congregation from which we had bought the building. It was a congregation of the Southern fundamentalist Church of Christ. They didn't know who was buying their building when they signed the contract and weren't happy when they found out. They were not going to give an extension or offer any grace to a gay congregation. At my first Board meeting, we debated if we should try to raise the money for the balloon note or simply begin looking for another place to which to move.

Perhaps worst of all, the late 1980s brought the devastation of the AIDS crisis to Middle America. Although the church only had 280 members at the time, during the third month after I arrived we had 18 funerals. Every death was a young man who only months before had been vibrant and alive. I was 33 at the time, and most of those who died were around my age. There were a couple of years when it felt as though everyone was going to eventually get sick and die, and there was nothing we could do but to bury them. I suspect only congregations in war zones or epidemics have ever faced such relentless loss with no time to grieve. Every Sunday, the prayer list stretched for pages with the names of those who were sick, hospitalized or dead. I remember one funeral for an elderly member where people were almost light-hearted simply because he had managed to make it to old age.

We trained dozens of lay people to do most of the hospital visitation. It was terrifying to someone if I actually came to visit them, because they assumed I was there to talk about their funeral. We tried assigning "buddies" to care for every person living with AIDS, but that soon became too overwhelming since support services were still quite limited. Even when people were hospitalized, our volunteers had to go three times a day to ensure that patients were fed. In those days, orderlies would leave food trays on the floor outside the patient's rooms.

Eventually, we created a program of teams of caregivers. These "care teams" became a model for many AIDS support networks around the country. At one point, we were caring for more than 800 people living with AIDS. We had two case workers and a fulltime AIDS chaplain. Our counseling center expanded from one part-time volunteer to

28 counselors trying to help young men cope with diagnosis or loss. We who survived suspended all feelings and simply forced ourselves to care for yet one more dear soul.

Early on, I realized our congregation couldn't possibly serve all the needs of the community living with AIDS, so we gathered neighborhood churches in an association. We held joint prayer and healing services at one another's churches. Then, when it was time for our church to host the service, the Roman Catholics refused to participate. When the Greater Dallas Community of Churches rejected our application for membership, the message was clear: we were on our own. Even in the face of death, grace was in short supply in the Church of Jesus Christ. Fundamentalists proclaimed AIDS to be God's punishment on gays. Regardless of how often I pointed out that most of the deaths in Africa were heterosexual, we still buried young men who were convinced God did not love them, and tried to comfort families convinced their loved one had gone to hell. No one will ever know the torment and suffering that fundamentalist pastors heaped on the dying.

Today, Dallas has several openly-gay elected officials, but, in those days, Judge Jack Hampton gave a lighter sentence to a murderer because, as Judge Hampton publicly declared, the victim was "only a gay man." Twice during those years the Ku Klux Klan came to our services in an attempt to intimidate our members. Operation Rescue disrupted our services and picketed us several times, as did Fred Phelps and his clan from Topeka. Phelps even picketed the funeral of a longtime member of our congregation who had died.

It seemed the logical thing, at that time, was to retool my ministry and steel myself to be a hospice chaplain. After six months in Dallas, I wrote to a friend that it appeared God had called me here to preside over the physical death of this church and community. While I myself am not infected with the virus that causes AIDS, I often went home at night exhausted and with a sense that I might not live through this crisis.

This description is offered so that you will have an accurate picture of the situation that we faced in those days. My ultimate purpose, of course, is to challenge you to consider if your situation can be nearly this bad. Let me be honest with you; if I had known the true situation in Dallas in 1987 God could not have dragged me by my hair anywhere near the state of Texas. I was not noble, brave or wise. I was ignorant. The two women talking in front of me at General Conference in Miami had no idea just how bad things really were for the Dallas Church. They had been right though; anyone who came to the Dallas MCC had to be out of their minds. While I didn't think I was when I accepted the challenge, I began to honestly fear that I soon would be. The emotional pressure was more than I thought anyone could bear. How could one think clearly enough to make good decisions, let alone provide vision, leadership and hope? Yet, I was sane enough to know that, short of a cure for AIDS, there was nothing this church and community needed more.

On the Sunday when I was a candidate for this church, the interim pastor led the congregation in prayer. They dimmed the lights and asked everyone to join hands. The small sanctuary was filled beyond capacity. There were no windows in the sanctuary, so the dimmed lights left us all together in almost total darkness. He began the prayer time by reviewing the recent additions to the church's prayer list. By the time we bowed our heads, even I was weeping, and I did not know a single person on that list. I realized that if ever there were a clinically depressed community desperate for a word of hope, it was this one.

As it turns out, that diagnosis was correct. While I might have been tempted to crush up some antidepressants in the communion wine, the real balm they needed was the authentic hope offered by the Gospel. It needed to be offered with compassion, passion and confidence. We had no time to wrestle with theological vagaries or to observe theological niceties. This was a community that needed the raw Gospel in heaping doses. Anything less and it would die. According to the testimony of many who survive HIV to this day, anything less and they would have physically died as well. Today, one of the most vigorous faith communities in America stands as a living testimony to the resurrection power of the faith in Jesus Christ.

In case you have missed it, here is my point again: if it can happen here, it can happen there. If it can happen to us it can happen to you. Weekly, people visit the Cathedral of Hope from all over the world and believe they have come to the Promised Land. They say we are most blessed, God's favored people. We believe that too, but we try never to forget that there was also a season when we felt like we had been abandoned and forgotten by God. We, who have lost so many and so much, bear witness to the truth of the resurrection and seek to offer that reality to others. Surely your wilderness is no worse than ours. Take our hands; there is a land of promise for you, too.

Chapter 3
20/20 Vision

Where there is no vision the people perish.
Proverbs 29:18

The wisdom of this proverb was never truer than it was for the Cathedral of Hope. Without a vision, this church surely would have perished, as would I, at least as a pastor. The Bible also says that those who lack wisdom should ask ... so I spent almost every night literally on my knees begging for wisdom. I felt entirely too young to be presiding over the death of a church that a community so desperately needed.

Somewhere in the course of this prayerful desperation, I came up with the idea of asking the people what they thought the vision of their church's future ought to be. Okay, so it wasn't a particularly brilliant or insightful idea, but it was the best I could come up with at the time. So, my partner Bill and I decided to invite every single member of the church over to our house for dessert and a chat with the new pastor. We divided up the membership roll and started with the letter "A." Every Friday night, 15-25 people showed up, probably only to see what the pastor's house looked like. Each week, we sat around on chairs and the floor, and the agenda was always the same. We started with the person to my immediate left and went around the room. Every single person had an opportunity to answer the same question: What do you believe God is calling our church to be or do?

People could pass when their turn came, but everyone had a chance to be heard. I sat and took notes. After each person had spoken, I thanked them and then tried to double check that I had heard them accurately. That exercise of reflective listening was revelatory just by itself.

At least once a night, people were startled to hear what they had just said. Somehow it was as if hearing it spoken aloud by the pastor made them clarify, question, expand and, often, reconsider what they really thought. I tried to conduct this exercise without critique, and, as it turned out, those gathered seemed to do the critical analysis for me.

It also became remarkably clear that, while they had never really talked about this topic among themselves, there was a shared set of core values. Surprisingly, week after week, each group articulated the same, relatively common, vision. This was far less likely in our church since it was only about 17 years old at that time. No one had grown up in our church, and we did not share a common denominational background. Apparently, my predecessor had done a good job laying a strong foundational identity.

While the theological and ecclesiological diversity of our church is unique, it is increasingly common and, I suspect, a trend for the future Protestant Church. Once upon a time, church growth experts held that one characteristic of growing congregations was homogeneity. If that were a rigid rule, however, our church would never have been able to grow. In surveys of each membership class at our church, about 24 percent of new members grew up in the Roman Catholic tradition. Ironically, about 26 percent grew up in conservative and evangelical Southern Baptist churches. What kind of church could possibly attract relatively equal numbers of Baptists and Catholics? While the majority of our congregation is lesbian or gay, we have discovered that we are far from homogeneous in any other way.

This reality is increasingly common in our culture and in our churches. Fewer and fewer people attend the church of their childhood. The cradle roll can no longer be relied upon to ensure a church's future. Large nondenominational churches have recognized and effectively exploited this reality. Many growing churches have removed their denominational labels from their name, discovering that identity screened out more people than it attracted. Almost no one on the street knows that the Crystal Cathedral is a Reformed Church, or that Saddleback Community Church is Southern Baptist. Fewer and fewer people seek out a church based on its denominational label. In addition, if someone has had a negative experience in a church sharing your label, that experience gets transferred to you and your church.

In recent years, the United Methodist Church and the United Church of Christ have both launched savvy media campaigns. Unfortunately, they can only advertise the denomination, and, ultimately, people attend the *local* church. All too often, what one sees on TV and experiences in the pew are quite discordant. The slick, fast-paced, creative media message sets people up to be disappointed by the reality they encounter in the local church they attend. The advertising efforts are certainly praiseworthy, but ultimately prove worthless unless the local church is prepared to change its vision of itself and its future to include meeting the needs of the unchurched and post-churched (those who grew up in church, became disenchanted and, ultimately, dropped out).

The people filling the pews of the largest and fastest growing churches in America are drawn from a wide range of mainline denominations and blended with a significant number of people who have no church background at all. While we may not share the theology or values of these churches, there are other lessons we can learn from them. It is deadly arrogance to dismiss them as having nothing to say to us—an attitude that will doom Christendom in America to become a fundamentalist and socially conservative faith.

How, then, do large, nondenominational churches create a cohesive functioning community that is, often, more diverse than many of our congregations in church background, economic status, race and gender? Like you, the Cathedral of Hope was clear that we would not use techniques such as fear or a common enemy to rally people and build a substitute for homogeneity. The only healthy replacement I could find was a unifying and compelling vision. Again, this isn't radically insightful, but it is amazing how often this gets overlooked by church leaders. Too often we assume that because we have our vision statement on our website or print it on our annual report, it is a part of the genetic make up of the body. That illusion is repeatedly shattered when conflict or crisis occurs.

The crisis had come upon us in the form of an epidemic that was decimating our membership and our community. This reality was a powerful factor in shaping what members of our church in the late 1980s thought our church's ministry should be. While we were clear that we were not an AIDS agency, we also knew that in this crisis we had a unique "product" to offer a people suffering from a terminal disease for which there was no cure and, at that time, no effective treatment. One young woman, who was the director of the local AIDS clinic, said to me and to those sitting in my living room one Friday night, "All I can do is treat people's symptoms and hope to prolong their life, but you have something to offer them that can heal them: hope." She went on to talk about the self-destructive behavior she too often saw, which she believed resulted from people being told they had no worth to God. The way the overwhelming majority of the church has historically treated lesbian, gay, bisexual and transgender people made it clear that there is no place for them in the family of faith or the heart of God. Robbing people of hope and the self-esteem that come from being God's beloved is murder. It kills the soul.

While few groups have been as overtly estranged as the gay community, make no mistake, there are thousands in your community who are living without hope, feeling alienated from God and God's family. Those people desperately need what your church has to offer. Are they part of the vision that shapes the identity of your congregation? You see, another reality that shaped our vision arose from the context of our ministry.

Living in the heart of evangelical America, many of our members have retained the urgency of their passion for saving people from the torment of hell. While we have come to define hell very differently than the churches from which we came, the urgency of our mission is no less real. The AIDS crisis focused this for us, but it also grew out of our own experiences. Many of us grew up in small towns where we felt crushing loneliness and isolation. The reality that a lesbian or gay teenager is three times as likely to attempt suicide is never far from our consciousness. The fact that these personal hells are made worse by, and in some cases created by, their local churches only adds to our sense of responsibility.

Coming from a small town in southern Georgia, these were all dynamics I understood and appreciated. What almost threw me off track, however, was the fact that this church was located deep in the heart of Texas. When people in the circle would talk about their vision that our church be large, I tended to discount it as a product of what I derisively called "Texas attitude." Several weeks had passed before a wise and erudite person I respected said bluntly, "I believe God has called us to be the largest gay church in the world and one of the largest churches of any kind." Stunned I asked, "Why?" She didn't hesitate but began to articulate how we had to be large enough and visible enough to change how people thought about LGBT people and how LGBT people thought about God.

Every person in the room nodded in agreement, and, across the room, one man, with tears rolling down his cheeks, began to talk about what a difference it would have made in his life to know that such a church existed when he was growing up. Others talked about how painful it had been to live for years feeling that God didn't love them. Soon the conversation was about how we could reach out to young people in small towns. It was the one meeting where our routine was sacrificed. In the weeks that followed though, when people talked about us being a large church, I was not so quick to dismiss them.

Once the congregation had been heard, I took my notes and went away to a bed and breakfast in East Texas that was owned by two members of the church. There, I spent days consolidating what I had heard and trying to assess what it meant. I also tried to evaluate the vision in light of the Gospel. I was disturbed by the conservative and sometimes fundamentalist language that had been used, but there was little I had heard that wouldn't find a home in the heart of Jesus.

Having consolidated the vision into a digestible list, I tried to find a way to summarize it. Ultimately, the three words "Cathedral of Hope" became my shorthand means of referring to the vision. When I returned from my retreat, I gathered the staff and other leaders I trusted and shared with them what my synthesis was and the summarizing phrase. The effect was stunning. In that small group, I saw the impact of hope being reborn. After a season when survival was constantly in doubt, to hear a vision for the future was healing and restorative.

The next test was to take the Board of Directors on a retreat and get their assessment. We went to the same bed and breakfast in deep East Texas. It was really too small for all of us, but, given our financial crisis, it was about the only place we could afford. In the parlor of that B&B we found the vision of the congregation resonating in our souls. During the last half of the second day, we invested deeply in a conversation about the need to reach out to LGBT people in rural isolation. In the late 80s, the only means we could discern for doing this was television, but we hardly knew how we were going to pay the light bill.

We continued our conversation as we went to dinner.

The owners of the B&B recommended a seafood restaurant that was located on a bayou about 20 miles from town. We drove out there talking all the way, until, at last, we literally ran out of road. At first, we thought we might be lost, but then we saw the sign that said "Uncertain, Texas." The sign noted a population of less than 100 as we turned off the paved road. Just down the way was the place where we would eat on the swampy shores of Caddo Lake.

It looked more like Louisiana than Texas, which is not surprising because we weren't far from the Louisiana border. The parking lot was full, though, and that is always a good sign when you are looking for food. The hostess seated us in the back room. We couldn't decide if it was because there were 10 or 12 of us or because she knew we really weren't from rural East Texas. As we got settled, our waiter appeared. He was, almost, the most obviously gay man I have ever encountered. After he had taken our drink order (iced tea was the strongest choice on the menu), he left the room, and we all spontaneously erupted in laughter.

I am sure we had a great meal, but what was most memorable was the waiter who proceeded to try and make a date with a single member of the Board. As we stood in the parking lot after the meal waiting to get back in the van, the young guy came out and asked us who we were. We hesitated for a moment and then told him we were the governing board of the Metropolitan Community Church of Dallas. His face lit up, and he began to tell us about a visit to our church some years before. Although he didn't say so directly, it was pretty clear that he had come home so his family could take care of him when he got sick. As he departed, he said casually, "You guys should start a church out here, 'cause you'd be shocked how many gay people there are."

The Board looked at me as if I had set all of this up for their benefit. I had not, but perhaps God had because we could not have gotten a clearer confirmation of the vision God had for this church. The waiter in Uncertain, Texas became a symbolic reminder in the consciousness of the church. As we pursued our vision, we did it as much for him as for us.

Telling stories like this one gives flesh to a vision. We have had to tell it over and over about people from places like Uncertain. We have had to tell it to new people as the church grew and as so many of our members from that time died. Together, we heard God call us to be a Cathedral — a large urban spiritual center, a church large enough to be an undeniably visible witness to and for LGBT people. Hope was what we had to offer, and it was, and is, something desperately needed.

From that day until this, every major decision we have made has been shaped and guided by this vision. Although we have had an occasional family conflict, this vision has brought together, and held together, a very diverse group of women and men. While the members of our congregation risk their jobs with every media exposure, we have deliberately been one of the most visible churches in America. When we moved into our current facility, it was just one week before Christmas 1992. CNN wanted to broadcast from our new building. One member who had joined the Board years after that initial retreat objected. Every other member, though, reminded her of the waiter in Uncertain, Texas. Although she was a major contributor and threatened to leave, the decision was never in doubt. We would be true to our vision, and that waiter, if he was still alive, would see us on CNN every hour Christmas Day, as they played an excerpt from our Christmas Eve service as a part of their headline news.

We did eventually develop a television ministry. Although it meant a legal battle, we even sponsored the first, and so far only, national broadcast by an LGBT organization. What we had no way of knowing in Uncertain was that the Internet would give people access to us in an amazing way. Hundreds of thousands of people visit the Cathedral online every year. We have been reported in every major newspaper in America and by many around the world. While we have not yet fulfilled our vision, it continues to motivate, unite and inspire us.

The world has changed since we began. Fortunately, it has changed for the better for gay people. We hope that we were a part of that positive change. While the Church is the place where change has come the most slowly, even there it has come. Today, the newspaper that serves the LGBT community in Dallas lists 27 churches that welcome gay people in one of the most conservative cities in America. As a result, our vision is evolving, but its importance is as great today as ever.

Chapter 4

Coming Out as Christians

It would not be an understatement to say that a miracle occurred at our church. A congregation that was depressed and dying literally took up its bed and walked again. No, most would say we ran and danced and laughed for joy. Resurrection became more than a theory to us.

The first thing we did was to hire a full-time AIDS minister. As it turned out, the church's music director had resigned just before my arrival. His incredible talent had shaped the worship and made it a major event every week. Without him, worship was struggling a bit, but I decided that, since we couldn't afford both, rather than replace him, we would use the funds to create a comprehensive AIDS ministry. We hired Rev. Paul Tucker, who was pastoring a church of about 150-200 people in Nashville. Paul was a seminary classmate of mine and a personal friend, so I knew he was the perfect person. We were clear that we did not want him doing pastoral care, at least not in the traditional sense. Rather what we needed was for him to build a congregation of 150-200 caregivers. No one human could do all that needed to be done in those days, and, besides, that is not my vision of how the Body is supposed to function. Too often the church has fallen into the trap of paying professionals to be in ministry while the members watch, encourage and pay the bills. Paul didn't need fans; he needed hands.

I must say that he did an amazing job, and this community will be forever in his debt. His competency allowed me, mostly, to relinquish that role. Soon, I was doing fewer and fewer pastoral visits, yet we ensured that every day a person was in the hospital they were visited. Lay people were even being asked to conduct funerals, because they were the ones who provided the direct ministry when the person was dying. It took a little work to put our egos aside and celebrate this as a success. One by one, our members began to come out of their closets and live out their Christian faith.

We pastors can get addicted to the adulation that comes from riding our white horses to a family's rescue when there is a crisis. In a role that provides many an opportunity for criticism, this is a place where we get lots of gratitude and appreciation. It is tough to give that up and empower the Body to authentically do this ministry. Yes, there were many times when it would have been easier just to do it myself, however that is not what I believe Jesus calls pastors to do. Our role is to "equip the saints" to be the Body of Christ in our community. When we are the "super-Christian," flying to the rescue in every crisis, what is really being served are the needs of our own ego.

Having gained this insight, a couple of years later, when we went looking for a new minister of music and worship, I shared what we had learned with the search team. Their first instinct was to go looking for the best possible musician, because we were at our best when our former director was with us. However, it was an artificial standard, because when he left, although the church had grown greatly, our overall music program had only deteriorated. This was because the music ministry had been built largely on his personal talent and incredible ability. What we really wanted this time was a leader who would build a program by which the *people* would make music, not the hired staff. We wanted a program in which, when the director left, the music would continue because it was our music, not theirs.

As a result, the committee found a new director who

did not play an instrument and was not really much of a singer. However, he was a genius at motivating, organizing and inspiring people. He soon built a music program that was, in its way, unmatched and that, a decade later, continues to make great music, even though this individual is no longer our music director. (He remains on staff as our webmaster.)

The AIDS crisis forced us to recognize this priority, but this is not a lazy approach to ministry. Recruiting, training, supporting and supervising ministry is hard work. However, if I have to personally provide pastoral care for every member of my congregation, then I cannot allow my church to grow beyond my own personal capacity. Time and again, pastors of a variety of denominations have subconsciously sabotaged, or at least resisted, the growth of their congregations because it threatened to outgrow their personal resources. Those women and men should be chaplains not pastors. A pastor's job is to equip the saints to do ministry, not to do ministry for, or to, a passive people. Too often we become the personal chaplains of private spiritual clubs.

At another Board retreat, a year or so after we visited Uncertain, Texas, we had a consultant come in to take us through a process of developing a comprehensive strategic plan. We had our vision; now, we needed a plan. The plan we developed turned out to be pretty worthless because we kept outgrowing it. The most helpful part of the whole process, though, was that this consultant asked us Peter Drucker's two defining questions:

1. What business are you in?
2. Who are your customers?

While the answers might seem obvious, we discovered that they were not, given our vision. While the first query was important and helpful, it was the second that offered to us a transformative "ah-ha."

As the governing body and the leadership of the church, our immediate response was that the membership was our customer base. After all, they are the ones who pay the bills and consume the product. However, remember what we said our vision was. In the light of that, it was the community—even the community in small towns beyond Dallas—for whom our "product" was intended. Our customers did not sit in our pews; rather, the pews were filled with the real ministers of the church.

Our vision was so great that it was beyond the capacity of the paid staff. We had no choice but to see ourselves as the equippers" of the ministers. Hence, at every membership class, we tell those who are going to join that we really don't need any more members. What we need are ministers. Their confirmation means that they are ready to "take off their bibs and put on their aprons." The confirmation classes are designed to be "orientation to ministry" classes. Every new member selects the areas in which she or he believes they can make a contribution. For a time, we had a sign over the main exit that said "Servants' entrance."

For almost two decades, at the beginning of every service, I have welcomed visitors and informed them that the real ministers of the church are those seated around them. At the end of every service, my benediction has been:

> *Our worship has ended, but **now** our service begins. Go from this place as the Body of Christ, for the whole world awaits you. So live passionately, and love faithfully, and celebrate every moment of your life from now until the finale, for the God of relentless grace goes with you. Amen.*

When people come to us from other churches, it takes some time to reorient them. The most powerful witness comes from the members themselves. A couple of years ago, a relatively new member was complaining to the person next to him in the pew about some component of a particular worship service. I am not sure if he disliked something we had started or the fact that we had stopped doing something else. Since we change our services dramatically with each liturgical season, it could have been either. However, when he said, "I don't like ..." the person in the pew replied, "Well, I don't think they did it for you. After all, we are not the customers here, are we? And if it benefits someone else, then I'm glad they made the change."

The concept of servant leadership is a lesson in which the Church of Jesus Christ needs a refresher course. Each congregation must come to see that serving the community where it lives is the only reason for its existence. Oh, I know the argument that we are a faithful remnant, etc., but, as my grandfather would say, "That is a pile of horse shit in the wrong place." The church is not a repository for theological orthodoxy, but a living expression of truth. Our job is not to defend the faith, but to express it to a hurting world. If what we believe is true, and in anyway meaningful, then it has to be relevant to a world on the verge of madness—a madness for which we bear some responsibility. If we know the truth or have a clue to the solution to the world's problems but withhold it in our stained glass repository then we bear as much guilt as any evildoer for the state of affairs.

Too many of our churches have become spiritual clubs that gather weekly for the sake of our members. Frankly, those churches should die so their property can at least be returned to the tax rolls. At least then they would be contributing to the greater good. While that may seem strong, it is clear that is not how Jesus lived and it is not how the Body of Christ must live. We must pry open our sealed windows and throw open our doors. We must reorient our life outward as servants of the Servant in deed and in truth. The first and most major reorientation must begin with the pastors and leaders.

The resurrection of our church began when we decided to equip our ministers to do hands-on AIDS ministry for those who did not even come to church. We soon were doing funerals for people who never darkened our doors, but to whom we had taken our ministry. Hundreds of people came to those funerals and saw an authentic church in action. Many of them came back and ultimately joined our community. Today, when we do surveys of new members asking when they first came to a service, most will say Easter or Christmas Eve. In those days the number one answer was "a funeral." While we did not intend this to be an evangelism tool, we discovered that any time we are authentically the Body of Christ people are attracted.

The church is never more vibrantly alive than when we are there for people in need. Just as thousands of people were attracted to the compassionate ministry of Jesus, so, too, a hurting world will find the unconditional compassion of a church radically appealing. I must have debated a thousand fundamentalist ministers over the years. It was kind of fun, frankly, because I had an unfair advantage. While for most of them it was a unique experience, there was nothing they were going to say that I hadn't heard a thousand times before. The major reason for these debates was that we were trying to fulfill our vision and take our word of hope into unlikely places where hurting teenagers might hear.

After a time, though, the debate grew tiresome, and, eventually, I simply said, "No." I didn't know if it was boredom or exhaustion. Then, one day, I saw a quote by Mother Teresa that resonated with what I was feeling. She was talking about the theological debates that have long raged in the Christian church when she said, simply, "Too many words. Just let them see what we do."

This quote stands beneath a bronze bust of Mother Teresa in our church. It became our theme. No longer would we try to argue that people could be lesbian or gay and Christian; we simply would be both of those things, visibly and proudly. The Cathedral of Hope is a younger, mostly middle-class congregation, yet for almost a decade we have given away more than $1 million in money, goods and services to those in need. The overwhelming majority of that has gone to children, and almost all of it to people outside our church and immediate community.

Just as our AIDS ministry became overwhelmingly oriented toward caring for others, so, too, our Community Outreach serves those who never attend the Cathedral. We provide tutoring, uniforms, health fairs, musical instruments, air conditioning, landscaping and supplies to four poor public schools. Not a single child in our church attends those schools, whose students are almost entirely Hispanic. We offer language courses and other support to the parents, as well as food and financial assistance. They don't attend our church, but they do bless us. They allow us to do what God has called us to do and to be whom God has called us to be. The church is constantly being recognized and thanked by the community and by city officials not because we are mostly gay or lesbian, but because we are living out our faith. Most of our members drive past dozens of churches to get to us because our servant ministry is congruent with whom they believe Jesus was.

In early 2006, the militant group Hamas won a huge upset in Palestinian elections. The Taliban in Afghanistan is making a comeback. Radical fundamentalist Islamic groups in Pakistan provided millions of dollars in assistance to earthquake victims. They say they are simply expressing the values of their faith. Perhaps, but what they are also doing is winning the hearts and minds of hurting people.

Whom do the hurting people in your community think of with gratitude? What is your church's reputation beyond your walls? What ministry do you have that is so winsome and moving that when a young couple moves into your community and starts asking about "good churches" even the neighbors who don't attend church are likely to tell them about yours?

A few years ago, an article appeared in the "Dallas Morning News" about the work that our congregation was doing with a local elementary school. One of our associate pastors went to a neighborhood diner for breakfast that morning. Sitting in the booth behind him were two men discussing the article. My associate couldn't help eavesdropping. He was amused to report that the older of these two guys, a man well past 70, concluded the conversation with this comment: "Well, I've never much cared for queers, but that bunch are real Christians."

The light from your stained glass windows is too dim to be seen through tears. You must reorient your ministry to equip the church rather than trying to be the church. You must reorient your members' ideas of service and whom the customer really is. Rather than **to** the church, it must be **through** the church to the world. We are not chaplains in a private club, but the equippers of the Body of Christ that gives its life for a hurting world.

Chapter 5

Meeting God's Longing and Ours

For most churches, Sunday morning worship is the "main event." There are congregations for whom small groups are the strong suit, and somewhere a midweek service is what draws people. However, for most of us, Sunday morning is the major point of contact for the majority of our members. It is certainly the number one point of contact for visitors/future members. Often when I teach church growth workshops, I say, "Growing a church is simple, but it is not easy." It is as simple as:

1. Getting people to attend.
2. Getting people to return.
3. Getting people to stay.

People visit churches for a wide variety of reasons: denomination, proximity, reputation, children's program, recovery support groups, etc. While none of us took a single seminary class in marketing, we should have. Today, 14 percent of Americans move every year. That means that almost every church has to attract a significant number of new people each year just to avoid significant decline. Of course, that rate isn't as great for people over the age of 65, but an older congregation has its own "transfer" problems.

So, how do we attract potential new members? Well, the easiest pool for potential growth is found in those who already visit our churches. At a workshop designed to reverse the decline of a congregation, I began by asking those attending what their average weekly attendance was. Of course, I already had those statistics, but it is interesting to gauge what a congregation believes about itself. Are they clear-eyed in their assessment, overly optimistic or overly pessimistic?

In this particular congregation, they were averaging 82 adults each week. They saw themselves as a very small church, but, in fact, they were just about average in terms of the size of churches in America. What I tried to get them to understand was that they had about as many resources as other churches. The question now was what would they do with them? It also helped them to see that, if they were to fulfill their vision for the church, they were going to need to substantially increase their numbers.

My second question to them was, "How many first-time visitors do you have each week?" Most guessed two or three, but the volunteer secretary for the church said that it was more like five to seven when you calculated Easter, Christmas and a couple of other big Sundays. Then I asked them to do a little math. "Take the lower number, which was five, and multiply it by 52." They were stunned to discover that 260 people visited their church each year. I then asked them to imagine what their church would be like if just half of those people came back again and ultimately decided to stay. It was an exciting thing to contemplate. They could more than double the size of their congregation simply by retaining half of those already visiting them.

Of course, that was the good news. The bad news was much harder to analyze. The courage to ask the next question is why congregations often need outside consultants: "Why aren't those people returning and joining?" Silence. The room was filled with satisfied customers, with people whose needs were being met. They loved their church and found it very painful to begin to consider why others would not love it just as much. Congregations sometimes know the answer but cannot bring themselves to articulate it. More often, however, the good people who fill our pews simply do not know why the place isn't packed each Sunday. Those who are most willing to do critical analysis are often those who are already unhappy or disgruntled.

Actually, the most accurate answers come from those who visit. It is important to ask new people what they like and don't like about us. They are fresh eyes, ears and hearts. What was it that brought them in the first place, and, more importantly, what was it that brought them back? What did they like about the service? What turned them off? What did they notice about the building? What bothered them? How many people spoke to them on their first visit? Did anyone remember them when they returned? Was the visitor packet helpful? Could they find the restrooms, and were they clean? On and on the list should go when we have an opportunity to get an objective evaluation.

I have never met a congregation that did not consider itself friendly. Their assessment is accurate, of course. They **are** very friendly **to one another**. However, that warmth rarely gets expressed toward, or experienced by, new people. In larger and urban churches the turnover is often so great that people can't tell the visitors from longtime members. This is exacerbated if your church has multiple services or if, like our church, you have lots of tourists visiting from out of town.

The more difficult, but probably more helpful, information about your church must come from those who visited but did not return. Quite likely, they will be hesitant to give you their brutally honest answer: the preaching or music was boring; the people were unfriendly; the bathrooms had a strange odor; the nursery was scary. Those are the most frequent answers people give in anonymous surveys, but they will rarely say that directly to people who care about their church deeply enough to ask. For many years, I have tried to take every guest preacher we have had to lunch after the service for a debriefing. They always have kind things to say about the church, and I thank them. Then I tell them that their kindness, while appreciated, is not really helpful. I need them to tell me what didn't work.

These guests are generally professionals who have insights that the average visitor might overlook. Dozens of times over the years, this kind of analysis has helped us improve the experience of those who visit. Let me give you an example about how we identified first-time visitors. We were a moderately sized congregation, and, at the beginning of each service, I would make announcements and ask first-time visitors to raise their hands so that the ushers might give them a gift and a guest packet. Seven or eight people would always raise their hands. It was a guest preacher, however, who first admitted that she would not have raised her hand had she been a first-time visitor. While she could preach to thousands, she was personally shy and didn't want to call attention to herself in a public setting. According to survey after survey, people are more afraid of public speaking than they are of death. Many healthy people are unwilling to risk what might happen should they publicly identify themselves to you in worship.

After our guest's comments, we began having everyone in the sanctuary register their attendance and simply asked the first-time visitors to give us their address so we could send them a letter and a gift. We did not single them out in anyway and told them exactly what we would do with the information for which we were asking. The first week the number of visitors we identified more than tripled. Even doing it this way, we estimate that we only identify about half of those who visit for the first time.

When we made this change, members complained that, since visitors didn't raise their hands, they didn't know to whom they were supposed to be friendly. I would pause when they said that and let them think about it. Then, if they didn't realize what they had said, I would remind them that the ideal solution is to try to be friendly with everyone, especially those we don't already know. Again, our decision about how to treat first-time visitors was based on remembering whom our customer is. Those who come to our service seeking God are the ones for whom we shape this and other parts of our service. They are the most important people to us, because without them our church has no future.

I have always thought that it would be an interesting exercise to take our bulletins to someone who has never attended church. What impression does our order of worship, the language we use and the overall document make to an un-churched person? Again, we who look at it week after week are not the best ones to make this evaluation. All too often our documents are filled with the "language of Zion." Insiders understand or, probably more accurately, are comfortable with this language. Visitors/seekers/future members often are made to feel uncomfortable, and even unwelcome, when they encounter insider language with no interpretation. Our congregation is genuinely ecumenical; hence, we have had to be keenly aware of the fact that even the most common language carries differing messages. For example, were we to simply publish in our bulletin the words "Lord's Prayer" we would find a cacophony of responses. A Methodist would pray "trespasses" while the Presbyterian prayed "debts." Complicating it still further is our congregation's commitment to inclusive language. Visitors are left to wonder what we do with "Our Father" and "Kingdom." Even our own congregation would be unclear since we try to live by principles not rules. There are seasons when we pray the Lord's Prayer from the *New Zealand Book of Common Prayer*. At other times we sing a call to prayer that addresses God as Mother and then pray the traditional Lord's Prayer addressing God as Father. The average church assumes that people know what is meant when they print the two words "Lord's Prayer." It is true that most of the members you have now do understand; however, unless we only want the church to exist for the life span of our current members, we must find a way to make outsiders into insiders. Avoiding insider language is a good place to start.

What other features of your service might make seekers and guests uncomfortable? What do you do every Sunday that is passively excluding? If our members are our customers then we should shape our service for them. However, if we genuinely want to be welcoming and inclusive, we must regard our guests as our most important worshipers. This does not mean we must abandon traditional worship. It simply means that we must help all who attend to understand and fully participate. It is amazing that, when we take the time to explain our traditions, those who have been longtime members are the ones who find it most meaningful.

One of the great traditions of our faith is hospitality and welcoming the stranger among us. Before introducing changes to our worship, it might be good to educate our members about that tradition and the implications. No congregation wishes to see itself as inhospitable, so they are much more likely to accept changes when they are being made in order to make others feel more welcomed into the family of God. The sacraments are an area in which this is most likely to be a factor. They are simultaneously the rituals to which longtime members are attached and the most mysterious and excluding experiences for our guests. Understanding the sacraments as means of evangelistic grace is a new idea for many, but it has its roots in the book of Acts. John Wesley thought everyone should be encouraged to participate in communion, because he believed it was a prime occasion for conversion.

Every component of a worship service should be shaped to bring new people in and to bring all people closer to God. Being attuned to the first-time visitor and making your service seeker-friendly has a remarkable byproduct. We discovered that people who had attended church all of their lives suddenly experienced ancient rituals and traditions in renewing ways. Repeatedly, old-timers reported learning things they didn't know they didn't know. In addition, it removes unidentified anxiety. Nothing ever happens in our services that is not explained and defined. There are no secret words, because everything is printed in the bulletin or on the screens. No assumptions are made, and, as a result, our members are never reluctant to bring visitors who have no church background.

Our best evangelists, of course, are new members, so growth becomes self-renewing. There are several reasons for this. Most significant, of course, is that new people are enthusiastic about having found somewhere that is important to them. They have yet to focus on the challenges every church faces but are still in the honeymoon phase of the relationship. The other important issue is that new members bring a new network of family and friends with them. While our long-term members love the church, after a few years of active involvement, most of their friends are their fellow members or people they have already tried, and failed, to bring to church. Also, they are far less likely to invite people to a church they have been attending for years. After all, if it was so great, why are they waiting until now to share it?

We encourage new members to invite their family and friends. They are given invitations to send to people inviting them to attend the service at which they will be confirmed. In addition, we have special services throughout the year, like Family Day or Friendship Sunday, that are specifically designed to motivate our members to invite people to church. One year, for Easter Sunday, we organized members of the congregation to invite friends and then host Sunday brunches following the service. That year, we filled the city's symphony center for two morning services.

Our Sunday services are passionately liturgical. We have a procession with acolytes, Eucharistic ministers and vested clergy. This may seem quite odd considering we are located in the city that has long been the bastion of conservative, evangelical Christianity. An Episcopal Bishop once leaned over to me in the middle of a service and said, "Isn't it deliciously ironic that in a homophobic diocese the largest Episcopal service is taking place here this morning." Our "high church" style seems out of place in the heart of Texas. It is true that the majority of our congregation comes from conservative, evangelical and fundamentalist backgrounds, but it is amazing how meaningful they find ancient rituals. Ash Wednesday, Maundy Thursday and Good Friday are days when people love to invite their friends to church. In those services, we seek to weave traditional elements with contemporary experiences. Frankly, sometimes it works, and sometimes it doesn't. Every service, though, is meaningful, well executed and memorable.

Within our worship, we often adapt contemporary praise and worship choruses to serve very traditional roles. They can work well as introits, graduals, glorias or choral benedictions. For example, we sometimes use Michael W. Smith's song "Ancient Words" as the gradual. The lyrics are:

> *Ancient words ever true*
> *Changing me, and changing you.*
> *We have come with open hearts*
> *Oh, let the ancient words impart.*

Holy words of our Faith
Handed down to this age.
Came to us through sacrifice
Oh heed the faithful words of Christ.

Holy words long preserved
For our walk in this world.
They resound with God's own heart
Oh, let the ancient words impart.

The words of the chorus are congruent with our theology, and they resonate with the congregation. Because it has a contemporary sound, a dusty piece of liturgy, like a gradual, becomes relevant again. The congregation understands that this piece of music is designed to prepare their hearts to hear ancient words in new ways.

While I am a weak singer, the congregation loves it when the pastor sings a part of the liturgy. I sometimes think they are secretly enjoying my pain, but what may be more true is that they see me becoming vulnerable and revealing that I am not a professional Christian who does all things well. Most commonly, the pastors of our church sing the consecration of communion, often responsively, or perhaps the invitation to communion.

The pacing of the service is another critical issue in the design of worship. If a service is all soft, gentle and passive the congregation is lulled into a passive compliant place emotionally. Regardless of what the liturgy or the preacher may say, the community gathered will lack a sense of urgency or vitality. On the other side, though, if the music is loud and the liturgy all passionate and bombastic the time of worship will leave the participants exhausted or anxious. Concerts, theater, musical recordings and even amusement rides understand the need to vary the pace, intensity and emotion to create a desirable experience. Worship planners should take note.

The rules of pacing differ from congregation to congregation, of course. Our tendency, unfortunately, is to design our services for those who are present and are in the majority. The result is that we may satisfy their needs, but not meet the needs of visitors who might be our future congregation. One Sunday in the early 1990s I was sitting on the chancel, and, while the choir sang, I made a startling observation. While I was nearing 40, I looked out over our congregation and noted that the majority of those present were in their early to mid-20s. I leaned over to the associate pastor (who was a decade older than me) and asked, "Where did all these young people come from?" Neither of us had even noticed the shift.

The next day over lunch, she and I had a long conversation about our sudden realization that the average age of the congregation was almost a decade or more lower than it had been when I arrived just four years earlier. She confirmed that the majority of our membership classes were all very young. We pulled the records of the two most recent classes and discovered that, in fact, they had averaged just over 26 years of age. The two classes numbered more than 60 people each, and we were holding seven confirmation classes a year. Not only were we younger, but we were growing rapidly.

Both realities were rather shocking because, at that time, we were worshiping in a terrible temporary facility while our current sanctuary was being constructed. Our worship space was horrific in almost every way, but no congregation would share space with us. So, we had very limited options. The room we used as a sanctuary comfortably seated about 250 people, but our attendance was nearly 700 a week. We sat in cheap and uncomfortable folding chairs. The ceilings were only nine feet high and covered with very effective acoustical tile. The air conditioning system was loud, and we had to supplement it with powerful fans to make it tolerable in the Texas heat. Unless every musician and speaker was loudly amplified, no one could hear a thing in that room.

As a result of the constraints of the facility, we had become compulsive about our pacing. The rule was that there could not be more than four seconds of silence at any time unless it was noted in the bulletin. Before the final note of a piece of music died away the person who would speak next was in place and prepared. When we prayed, the choir remained standing, poised to begin their anthem. In evaluating the change, we discovered several things:

- No one is edified watching someone walk into place. If our worship time is precious and holy, why waste it with actions that are not?
- On radio or television repeated silent pauses would get someone quickly fired. When did we decide that what we do deserved any less thought and preparation?
- Young people who grew up on television and radio subconsciously interpret unnecessary pauses as unprofessional and, therefore, unimportant.
- A fast-paced service or, at least, one that seemed deliberately paced, kept the congregation's interest and seemed congruent with other important experiences in their life, since they had experienced almost every important event via television.

Ancient liturgies presented with energy, intensity and passion can be as attractive and powerful for young people as for older. We discovered that it wasn't about volume or dramatics; it was about pacing and treating every component as though it were important and worthy of their attention. Reading scripture like it is a love letter from God can allow those who have heard it all their lives to hear it anew and allow those new to church to fall in love with the scripture. If we present it like we have read it a thousand times and is threadbare, then who can fault people for losing interest? If, however, we prepare people to hear it (a gradual spoken or sung) and celebrate it having been read (a Gloria) then everyone knows something holy has taken place in their midst.

> *I love to tell the story*
> *For those who know it best*
> *Seem hungering and thirsting*
> *To hear it like the rest.*

When the gospel is presented with energy and passion, and worship authentically connects people with God, everyone's needs are met. Soon, those who are in our pews will need to slide over to make room for those whose hearts still long for the divine. We must reach a generation that thinks our churches are the last place where they will encounter God. If we make worship passionate and meaningful, rumors will begin to spread, and they will come to see and hear for themselves. That is our future, but it will not come if we only meet the worship needs of those who are already present. We must figure out what must change in order for us to meet the needs of those who have not yet arrived. If we do not hurry, when the current generation filling your pews is gone, the church will be too.

Chapter 6
21st-Century Liturgy

One way we seek to bring our service into the 21st century is through the use of multimedia and multi-sensory experiences in worship. Most progressive or mainline denominational folk seem to think that this is the domain of contemporary, conservative mega-churches. The facility we now occupy was designed by us, and we were the general contractors. Back then, few church builders in Texas were interested in building a facility for the world's largest lesbian and gay congregation. For good or for bad, we have no one to blame the design of our facility on but ourselves.

Amazingly, the debate over what the building would look like and how it would function was remarkably civil. Long before the process began, we identified the values that the congregation wanted to have reflected in the building. Ironically, they were not what one might generally think a mostly lesbian, gay, bisexual and transgender church might desire. Our architecture is pretty simple and traditional, and our morning services very liturgical. We have a center aisle with pews on either side, stained glass and a giant 35-foot stone cross in the front. While the building was being constructed, the congregation worshiped in a temporary facility and chose the name "Cathedral of Hope." That choice shaped many future choices. The phrase, which was a shorthand reminder of our vision, soon became our identity. I should probably confess that while we were worshiping in a squatty, ugly office building painted glow-in-the-dark-pink I refused to let them use the name "cathedral" publicly.

Our worship became more formal when we moved from the temporary space, which was cramped and small, to our permanent home, which felt enormous. Each week, in the two main services, there is a procession with a crucifer, torch bearers, word bearer, half a dozen acolytes and Eucharistic ministers robed in cassocks and surplices. At the end are pastors and liturgists robed in albs and stoles, followed by the Dean and the Rector in albs and chasubles. In some seasons our services also include a thurifer and an abundance of incense, as well as clips from a television show that was just aired on Friday night.

While we follow the lectionary and the liturgical calendar through the year as rigidly as if we were high church Episcopalians, we illustrate it by using a variety of elements from pop culture. Let me offer some examples:

1. When the "Matrix" movies were first popular they offered a plethora of theological illustrations. In the first film, the main character, Neo, was offered a red pill or a blue pill—the choice to awaken or continue the illusion in which he lived. One Sunday, we used clips of the movie in the sermon as illustrations, and we also gave everyone in the congregation a tiny cellophane bag in which we placed a red jelly bean and a blue one. The sermon was about our need to resist assimilation and awaken to our true identity as children of God. We concluded by offering the congregation a choice of which pill to take, complete with the warning that life could forever change.

2. In another sermon series we focused on the will and grace of God. The TV series "Will and Grace" offered the illustrations. Another time we used the cable series "Six Feet Under" to talk, honestly, about the issue of death and dying. In our Texas culture, we were able to do a very popular series called "Life

Lessons from Country Music." While the music was done live in the room, we used, as a backdrop, clips from the music videos, which we borrowed from our neighborhood country-western bar. "The X-Files" well illustrated a series called "The X-mas Files." We also have used "The Amazing Race" to illustrate spiritual principles in much the same way Paul used athletic allusions. "Life Lessons from Lucy" was a huge hit, and we discovered just how many people knew the "Vitameatavegamen" routine almost by heart.

3. We don't use just video clips. For a sermon about the bread of life, we baked bread all morning and used fans to blow the scent into the sanctuary. For a sermon in which we used the fact that peach trees require a freeze to bear fruit, we used peach-scented room deodorizer to set the mood. When the Gospel lesson is the story of Jesus calling Peter the rock, why not give small pebbles to everyone when they arrive?

4. One fall we did a long series called "Spiritual Geography." Using various means, we tried to "take" the congregation to a different nation or culture every week. We started off talking about Celtic Christianity and used Irish and Celtic music, symbols and video images. The week we visited Greece, we looked at the theological issues unique to the Orthodox churches. The sanctuary reeked of incense when people arrived, and we gave every person a card with an icon. The youth sold baklava afterwards. At the beginning of the series, we gave everyone "Passports," which we stamped when they arrived at church each week. If they were present six of the eight weeks they qualified for a drawing for two roundtrip airline tickets, which we got donated. A woman guide modeled after "Indiana Jones" made an appearance during the

announcements each week to describe the places we would visit that day. Ultimately, it was all a fun way to get people to have an open mind about profound spiritual lessons that we needed to learn from other cultures.

5. A Lenten series called the "Art of Discipleship" featured classic art or an artist as the entry point for the theme each week. Again, we followed the assigned readings, but we illustrated them with a different artist. The week we did Vincent Van Gogh people arrived to find "Starry Night" on the cover of the bulletin and as the background on the screens, as well as Josh Groban singing that song made popular years ago by Don McLean.

6. A particular favorite of our congregation was the time we used Broadway musicals as the basis for a sermon series. Music was easy to perform or play, and we discovered that a good number of the most popular musicals had been videoed or turned into movies. We also got people to sing who had been in a performance of the musical, perhaps in college, or who were part of a tour that happened to be in our vicinity. The sermon I did using "Les Misérables" remains an all-time favorite to this day. The Gospels hardly have a better illustration of the contrast between fundamentalistic legalism and grace.

This list could go on and on, but my point is that being creative and contemporary is not precluded by having formal or traditional worship. While considerably more informal than we are, the folks at Ginghamsburg United Methodist Church (www.ginghamsburg.org) probably have the best-known multimedia worship of any mainline church. They have written a couple of books to help others learn how, and they host annual conferences. Of course, this is just the next step in what Robert Schuller and the folks at the Crystal Cathedral have been doing for decades. They were major inspirations in how we thought about church in many ways, and their annual leadership conference is still worth the trip.

For us, making use of multimedia in worship was a matter of starting small and growing. Cameras and projectors are expensive, but, daily, they are falling in price. Today, you can buy the whole system for what we paid for our first camera, and we bought our whole system for half what the Crystal Cathedral paid for a single camera. If you are not going to broadcast your services the cost and complexity is considerably reduced. While television airtime remains prohibitively expensive for most of us, cable access is virtually free, and the Internet has made our services accessible virtually around the world. Currently, more people worship with us via the Internet than fill the sanctuary at any given service. We believe membership in our on-line congregation will only continue to grow in the future. Viewership for cable access is small, but they estimate that an average of 2,000 people see every broadcast. Few of us have that many people in our sanctuary each week.

A laptop and a projector can do wonders for bringing a service into the 21st Century. For younger and contemporary people, they can provide the stained glass of their generation. The Internet provides millions of readily available images that can enhance worship and preaching. Although most of us are familiar with computer programs and Internet access, many of us are not. Venturing into this area provides a great opportunity to enlist the assistance of a group of young and enthusiastic volunteers. What an amazing opportunity to recruit and empower a whole new segment of the population into the sacred work of worship. Nearly 200 million, mostly young, people are on MySpace (www.myspace.com). How can you recruit some of those young people to create a space within your church that belongs to them?

While many preachers who use multimedia in worship rely heavily on PowerPoint presentations to communicate, my sermons tend to be much more inductive and do not lend themselves to that structure. I do love being able to show a picture of the person I am quoting or about whom I am telling a story. That has often allowed me to bring the faces of women, African-Americans, Native Americans and others who were under-represented on the chancel into worship without my needing to point out the race or gender of an author. Talking about the cost of war is one thing, but an image of children begging for food in front of a missile silo made the point much more persuasively than I ever could. I am very auditory, but many people are visual. A random image of a fisherperson casting a net can give the congregation access to an ancient parable that Jesus told.

In addition, by using quotes on the screen, people who are more visual than auditory stay engaged longer. Even auditory folks are helped if the quote is complicated. There are quotes I use now that I would not use if I was solely dependent on people to hear them alone. In seminary, I was taught how to use my voice to create the illusion of underlining something or placing it in quotes. That is much easier when you are able to put on a screen the point you seek to emphasize. I often read authors who cite movies or television episodes as illustrations. Each time we do that in sermons, we are able to pause and allow the medium to tell its own story much more effectively. I once described the chaos of Jesus cleansing the temple. While I talked, playing on the screen was a silent video of a modern movie's depiction of that scene. It showed Jesus' anger much more effectively than my description could. When I quote the lyrics of a song, frequently we will play the music quietly in the background.

In addition to sermon aids, multimedia serves us well in other ways. For example, while we have our own hymnals, we actually print hymns in our bulletin. This allows us to vary our selection more effectively and to always ensure the language is inclusive. We also put the words on the screen, which allows the congregation to raise their heads when we sing. The sound, as many a guest preacher can testify, is amazingly powerful. At the end of communion, as an act of thanksgiving, the congregation rises, joins hands and sings a familiar chorus of praise. It is impossible to hold a hymnal and your neighbors' hands at the same time, but when the words are on the screen even first-time visitors can join in fully.

With multiple services, when we announce that we confirmed new members at the earlier service, the folks who come later get to actually see a bit of that event and the faces of the newest members. When we thank volunteers who spent the previous day running a health fair, building a Habitat house or cleaning up a neighborhood, we can show actual footage of those we are thanking. Those images greatly assist in recruiting volunteers for the next project. That footage also serves us again when we review the year or mourn the loss of one of those volunteers who has died.

Through the use of multimedia, great leaders, living and dead, have spoken to our congregation. One year, when we gave our "Hero of Hope" award to the United Church of Christ for their stand on behalf of the rights of same-gender couples, their president, John Thomas, was able to speak to the congregation, even though he was out of the country at the time. Another year, we presented the Hero of Hope award to Congressman John Lewis. Telling the story of Congressman Lewis being beaten as a young man on the bridge to Selma is one thing, but actually showing footage of that scene brought young people to tears and was the most powerful way we could introduce him before he spoke. Rather than quote Dr. King's sermons, it is much more powerful to let him actually deliver a bit of it in the room.

We are seeking to communicate with a generation of people who have seen every major event in their lives (including, in many cases, their own births) on TV or video. While many of us may see watching TV as a passive behavior, the death and funeral of Princess Diana of Wales first revealed a whole new reality of global connection and participation that did not require one to be present. Dr. Leonard Sweet, in his book *Post-Modern Pilgrims*, writes about how our culture has replaced the written word with visual images as the main source of experience and learning. It is not our message but the medium that must change if we are to communicate effectively with a new generation.

My underlying point is the fact that the church must learn to use technology as effectively as other organizations. We cannot pretend that we are the master communicators any longer. Dr. Fred Craddock taught me to tell stories, and that skill has served me well. But I have had to learn to use multimedia to tell stories in whole new ways. Attracting un-churched people into the community and communicating with the iPod generation requires that we develop new ways of telling an old story. William Butler Yeats said, "An education is not the filling of a pail, but the lighting of a fire." The same is true of our preaching and worship. People are seeking an experience with God, not more information about God. The church must become the facilitator of those experiences, rather than a library where their history is preserved.

Chapter 7
God Got Your Tongue?

Last night I met a parishioner at Starbuck's. Frankly, after a long day, by 9 p.m. I would have just as soon met him for a drink, but you see that was part of the problem. After about 10 minutes of talking, I wanted to drown him in his Venti Skinny Latte ... with my best pastoral compassion, of course. He spent the first 10 minutes of our conversation stringing together almost every 12-step cliché I had ever heard. He had been going to Alcoholics Anonymous/Narcotics Anonymous meetings every day and had the program memorized and the language perfected. The only problem was he was still not sober.

That encounter could be a parable of how the church too often responds to the deep hurts of those we are called to serve. We have the program memorized and the language perfected, but, somehow, we never quite manage to connect in a transformative or healing way. There are two linguistic habits I find in the church that have the capacity to make me an atheist. Both of these seem to impact the effectiveness of our well intentioned ministry.

One was demonstrated on an NPR program I heard on which a well-educated, liberal pastor was being interviewed. Repeatedly, she would string together religious clichés and "psychobabble" that clearly drove the interviewer nuts. She had to *reflect back* every caller's question to make sure the person *felt fully heard*. She always *validated* their perspective before almost apologetically offering an *alternative view*. Then she would *unpack* the issue for the audience. She would conclude her remarks by reminding the caller that *it is the process that has value* and that the caller needed to *stay on the journey*. Half the time I couldn't tell if I agreed or disagreed with her position. After a few minutes, though, I knew I really didn't care. Her liberal-psychobabble-religious-speak made it clear that she didn't really care about the callers because she was living in a world all her own. If she lived in the real world with the rest of us she would have learned our language. If she really cared about us, she would have spoken **to** us, not **at** us in language no one in real life actually uses.

Pastors need to put down their exegetical work and self-help books and go have a cup of coffee at the local diner. We must escape our ivory towers and learn again to speak the language of normal people. They get "pissed," not "incensed." They are "afraid," not "anxious." Normal people "make friends;" they don't "build community" or, worse yet, "have fellowship." People are struggling to pay their bills, keep their kids off drugs, and hold their relationships together. They don't want to "partner with you." They want to hear a word of hope, plainly spoken in the language that they use every day by someone who believes it themselves and cares about them. Are we really so insecure about our station in life that we still need to prove to people that we actually have a graduate degree? Frankly, they don't care. What they want to know is if you care about them. Talking down to them by using language they don't use isn't a way to show our love or articulate God's grace.

Jesus was a genius at this very thing. He was a learned, intelligent rabbi, but he told stories people could relate to about things they knew all about. In the words of Brennan Manning, Jesus was "a stranger to self-hatred," so he didn't need to impress anyone with his wisdom and knowledge. Jesus' only agenda was to connect with everyone he encountered and reach them where **they** were, not where He was. No wonder "the common people heard him gladly," while the religious intellectuals dismissed him completely. When we talk about subjects the average person doesn't really care about and use language that isn't used outside the church or academia, we have abandoned the value system of Jesus and the people of God's heart.

Jesus didn't help Mary and Martha "process their pain" after Lazarus died. He cried with them. He didn't try to "reinforce the self esteem" of the woman taken in adultery; He pronounced her forgiven, lifted her up, and sent her on her way to live again. Jesus didn't quote scholars that no one had ever heard of in order to impress his listeners with his knowledge, but He "spoke as one who had authority." Jesus didn't use illustrations that proved He had a seminary education, but He talked about scattering seed, and lost sheep, and children who disappoint. Jesus seemed to think that if God had possession of a teacher's tongue s/he would speak plainly words of grace, healing, challenge and hope in a way that everyone could understand, not just the religious authorities.

The other linguistic habit of the church that makes me want to drink is that we use what we sometimes call "the language of Zion." That is, all too often we use terms that only insiders understand, or, perhaps more accurately, we use terms that only insiders use and **nobody** really understands. Although I'd rarely recommend a book by Intervarsity Press, it might be helpful if we all read *God Talk: The Triteness & Truth in Christian Clichés* by Randall J. VanderMey. It also would be a great exercise to make an insider vocabulary list. Start with "A." Here are a few of my favorites:

Abide
Abundant
Abundant mercies
Accept Jesus
Accept the Lord
Admonition
Ask Jesus into your heart
Amen!
Ascension
Atonement
Atoning blood
Authority

You can probably add many to my A list. The point is we use many words that are never heard in ordinary life. The effect is to exclude people who are not already insiders, to distance our message from real life and real people, and isolate us from the people who need us most. Many decades ago, Harry Emerson Fosdick was reported to have chided his colleagues by accusing preachers of being the only people in the world who believed that people got out of bed, got dressed and made their way to church because they were, "Desperately anxious to discover what happened to the Jebusites."

If it is our true agenda to reach people other than those who already attend our church then we must diligently purge from our vocabulary insider language that excludes. Now, that is not to say that we cannot teach people about "atonement," for example. It does mean that we shouldn't assume that they know what we mean when we say that word, or that everyone shares a common definition. We must say what we really mean and carefully define any terms that might not be used in a person's daily life.

Admittedly, perhaps all professions are bad about insider language, but I think people who work for denominations must hold PhDs in the use of terms and abbreviations that no one but the consummate insider would use. I laughed out loud when I read a press release announcing the news that our congregation had joined the United Church of Christ (UCC). It said, "In accordance with the denomination's grassroots governance style, issues related to congregational standing and ministerial authority are dealt with at the Association level." I laughed because the release was written by a dear friend, and it probably never crossed his mind that the average person reading that sentence in their weekly paper would have no idea what any of it meant. It was no surprise that almost no one picked up the press release. When the Church talks about synods, diocese, conferences, collegiums, standing and associations it is speaking to itself. That is perfectly appropriate in many settings, but public statements should not leave the reader feeling ignorant, uninformed or excluded. Any time we do that we violate our core values.

So, how then should we speak? The answer depends not so much on whom your listeners are, but on whom you **want** your listeners to be. Are we talking to ourselves alone and expecting no "outsiders," newcomers or seekers to be listening? There are meetings, classes and programs in which insider language is perfectly acceptable, but public worship is not such an event. It is easy to fall into the trap of thinking that "everyone" knows what we mean when we use certain phrases. The problem is the exceptions to that are the people who most need what our churches have to offer, and they are the people that our churches most need if we are to have a future. While I do not believe that "build it and they will come" applies to church facilities, I do believe that phrase from the movie "Field of Dreams" applies to church communication. We must speak the language of the people we **hope** to reach, not the language of the people who are already a part of our family. I remember making an announcement years ago about some activity of the "UMW." Later, at the door, a woman who was a professor at a local college and a first-time visitor remarked that the event sounded interesting and asked if only the men of the church could attend. Something in how I made the announcement, or perhaps in how she understood church, left her with the impression that the abbreviation UMW stood for the men of the church. I explained that UMW stood for United Methodist Women. She turned red-faced and laughed at her misunderstanding and made some remark about how the initials sounded like a labor organization. My explanation only served to make her feel foolish and even more like an outsider. The fault was entirely mine, and she never visited again.

Not using insider language and abbreviations seems very apparent, but a sampling of church websites, newsletters and worship services proves it is a greater challenge than we might think. Equally challenging is discovering new strategies for effective communication. Perhaps it would be helpful to draw on the lessons of another institution if we are to be proactive in our communications. George Lakoff is a professor of linguistics and cognitive science at the University of California, Berkeley. He is also a fellow of the Rockbridge Institute, which works to teach progressive people to communicate more effectively in the public debate. Professor Lakoff is the author of the best selling book *Don't Think of an Elephant* in which he seeks to teach progressives to reframe political issues in order to be more effective in communicating with the average American. While his lessons are about political values and positions with which we might agree or disagree, I believe his strategy and insights are as helpful for spiritual progressives as for political progressives.

Lakoff begins by asking why fundamentalists and religious conservatives hold the particular values they do. For example, what does cutting taxes have to do with opposing gun control? Or, how does being "pro-life" connect to supporting capital punishment and a stronger military? The Religious Right, essentially, has become monolithic in their support of particular political and social positions that, to an objective observer, might seem completely disparate. Honesty, however, compels us to acknowledge that the same is true with progressives as well. For example, most often we support abortion rights and oppose capital punishment without a hint of conflict. The question here is not really which position is "correct" as much as how they become connected in our common thinking.

Dr. Lakoff suggests it is rooted in our understanding and experience of family systems and dynamics. In particular, he identifies the models of the "strict father" or the "nurturant parent" dichotomy. According to this aspect of his theory, political and social conservatives predominantly hold to the strict father world view that is authoritarian and hierarchical, with clear lines of good and evil. The strict father model begins with a set of assumptions:

> *The world is a dangerous place, and it always will be, because there is evil out there in the world. The world is also difficult because it is competitive. There will always be winners and losers. There is an absolute right and an absolute wrong. Children are born bad (sinful), in the sense that they just want to do what feels good, not what is right. Therefore they have to be made good. What is needed in this kind of a world is a strong, strict father who can:*

> - *Protect the family in the dangerous world,*
> - *Support the family in the difficult world, and*
> - *Teach his children right from wrong.*

> *What is required of the child is obedience, because*
> *the strict father is a moral authority who knows*
> *right from wrong.*

Professor Lakoff goes on to discuss the link between this family dynamic and free-market capitalism. Adam Smith, an 18th-Century Scottish political economist and moral philosopher, viewed capitalism as everyone pursuing their own profit. A good/moral person is someone who is disciplined enough to obey the rules and succeed/prosper. Do-gooders screw up the system by trying to help someone who is not disciplined enough to help themselves. People adhering to this worldview see social programs designed to help people as not only misguided, but morally wrong.

Conversely, progressives are guided by a more nurturant parent ideal, which allows for conversation, diversity and ambiguity:

> *Both parents are equally responsible for raising*
> *the children. The assumption is that children are*
> *born good and can be made better. The world can be*
> *made a better place, and our job is to work on that.*
> *The parent's job is to nurture their children and to*
> *raise their children to be nurturers of others.*

All the social programs supported by progressives grow out of this worldview that values fairness and responsibility

While acknowledging the inadequacy and over-simplification of this generalization, Lakoff suggests that these two realities "frame" the various value-based decisions that we all make. Ultimately, he uses this frame to explain why logical arguments alone prove inadequate. He suggests that people are more prone to vote their identity than even their self-interest.

What is particularly helpful in this for us is to

understand that, if we wish to have our message heard in an empathetic way, when we seek to communicate with people we must do so within **their** world view. To say that another way, this theory of communication acknowledges the reality that the overwhelming majority of thought is subconscious not cognitive. The liberal/progressive church too often has assumed that additional information and rational argument is sufficient to persuade people of the validity of our worldview. Rationalism is often the frame of those with a nurturant parent view of God. It is our arrogance, however, that causes us to forget that everyone does not share our view or causes us to believe that those who do not share our view are mistaken and simply need to be taught the error of their ways. We miss the power of symbol and metaphor and the emotional resonance of certain words or phrases rooted in our family systems.

For those who see life within the framework of a strict father family dynamic, God is understood as punitive, punishing those who disobey. Jesus balanced the scales of God's justice for those who accept Jesus as the moral authority, or Lord, over their lives and, therefore, obey. For the nurturant parent crowd, grace is the metaphor for God's ultimate nurturing goodness in us.

How, then, do we speak to people whose frame differs from ours? Well, according to Lakoff, former President Bill Clinton succeeded by "stealing the other side's language." That is, he spoke to them with phrases that resonated with their own values. In our case, it may be helpful to remember that, while we do not have a high value for concepts like hell, there are millions who are spiritually motivated by avoiding that fate. It has been my own experience that, in a culture dominated by fundamentalists and evangelicals, speaking of hell has great power. Doing so with integrity requires me to frame a new definition, but it is easy enough to identify a number of ways in which the human soul is sentenced to hell by alienation and estrangement. There are no shortages of hells about which we can speak: loneliness, fear, isolation, guilt, etc. Each week, in the ritual of communion, we can talk about people coming forward to receive Jesus again. Clearly, many of the characters and authors of the Bible shared the fundamentalist's strict father view of God. That gives us tools to gain a hearing and then help people reframe their understanding of God.

Because Christian fundamentalists have dominated the media for a generation, they have successfully defined the Christian faith for the average American. Seminary-educated clergy do not tend to listen to televangelists or radio preachers, and we forget that other people do. Dr. James Dobson has convinced millions of Americans that God is a strict, though benevolent, Father and, hence, the model of how the religious life is to be understood. Since he is not a feature on NPR, we might miss the fact that he has sold millions of books and the response to his daily radio show is so great that he has his own zip code. When we fail to hear and understand what people are listening to, we cannot understand how they hear and understand what we are saying. In our intellectual confidence, we assume that everyone understands that what media fundamentalists are selling is just one brand of the Gospel. We know that what they teach has, in other ages, been considered by theologians to be deficient and even heretical, and we operate as if the whole culture is aware that this is the case. After all, no one believes everything they are told by the media, do they?

Unfortunately, the media-savvy fundamentalists know that they have already won a great victory: They have framed the argument. They own the religious assumptions in the popular culture. Perhaps their greatest victory is that they have redefined Christianity without us even knowing it. We keep using language that **they** have defined and are clueless why people do not understand what we mean.

We now must persuade people that their understanding of the Gospel is not universally, nor historically, held by most Christians. Mainstream, Protestant Christianity is now an alternative version of the truth to the majority of Americans. My own children believe that the Southern Baptists are the majority and that their belief is the standard. They were shocked to learn that, in the scope and history of Christendom, evangelicals are actually a small minority who simply have learned to behave as though what they believe is the standard of orthodoxy.

Few people actually know what the Bible says, or what Jesus taught, so the prooftexting they hear through the media or at the occasional religious service provides them with most of their understanding of orthodoxy. In addition, the Religious Right's ability to seamlessly weave their social conservatism with their theology has provided many marginally religious people with an understanding of Christianity to which there is only a faint alternative. They have successfully framed the argument, but "mainline" clergy still do not know that we are now the counter-culture messengers within our own faith.

Professor Lakoff and his colleagues suggest that for progressive politics to ever regain power, progressives must learn from the conservatives how to create a frame within which people are able to hear, understand and empathize with their message. So, too, the progressive church must learn both to understand the religious framework the average un-churched person lives in and communicate with them by using words and images that address people where *they* are, rather than where *we* are. We must begin by reclaiming words that have been redefined by fundamentalists. Let me offer another tangible example with which we have struggled.

In our attempt to use gender-inclusive language, our church ceased to talk about God as our "Heavenly Father."

It makes perfect sense to us that since God is not a human male we need to use language to address God that is less restricted and that communicates a broader understanding. For years, we began the Lord's Prayer by saying "Our God," or perhaps "Our Creator," or maybe "Our Parent." All of these seem more accurate ways to address God. We managed to remove gender from all of our language, both about humans and about the Divine. In a class at our church, I once heard someone say that, at our church, they had learned that "God is neither male nor female." As I pondered that statement, I realized that an important point had been missed. Our goal had not been to teach that God was neither, but, rather, that God was **both**. Gender is a divine gift, and it is part of what it means to be created in the image and likeness of God.

That incident compelled me to examine what had been lost as we removed gender from our God-talk. Our congregation's passion is to teach people that, far from being a source of sin and shame, human sexuality is a divine gift. By rendering our Creator as without gender, we had undermined that teaching. Further, when I listened to the prayers of my conservative sisters and brothers, I realized that there was a passion and intimacy that prayers around our place often lacked. While there is great danger in anthropomorphizing God, there is also a gift that can be lost when we become deist in our language. The return of sexism where the masculine is deified and the feminine obscured was not an alternative for us. Although we continue to struggle with the issue, it is now a conscious struggle. We are alert to the danger of speaking of God in remote and intellectual language that is inaccessible for the average person. Today, we pray the Lord's Prayer saying "Our Father" but we find other ways to bring gender balance to our worship's images of God.

Jesus instructed us to love God with all our "heart, soul, mind and strength." Progressive churches will never attract people so long as we only seek to help people access God with their mind; heart, soul and strength (passion) must all find equal place in our worship and communication. How do we frame the faith in such a way that people feel our message emotionally and connect to God with their hearts? How do we help people integrate their faith into their core, into their very souls? And how do we create for people a sense of urgency, relevance and passion so that their faith has the strength of life itself? Christian fundamentalism has learned to answer those questions, leaving the purely intellectual appeal to the mainline denominations. It is my conviction that this issue, more than any other, explains the decline of most of our churches and denominations.

Jesus was called Rabbi or teacher, but he told stories directly out of the life experience of those who listened to him. He touched them where they were hurting. He celebrated with them in their joy and wept with them in their grief. The passion of the One who overturned the tables of the money changers seems completely missing from most mainline churches today. It is no coincidence that the crowds that flocked to hear Jesus are also missing. We do not have to abandon our intellect and education, but, if we do not learn to also connect with the hearts and souls and passion of people, we will continue to watch the fundamentalist churches grow and their definition of the Christian faith prevail.

A few years ago, I was present in a worship service in which the preacher actually yawned in the middle of his own sermon. That seemed a perfect symbol of too much of what passes for worship in our churches. If we do not find ourselves moved, inspired, challenged and motivated by our worship, why on earth would we expect others to be? Time is a more precious commodity than money these days. No one will carve time out of their busy schedule for church today unless, or until, they are relatively confident that they will have an encounter with God there. Learning more about religion or God won't motivate people to fill your sanctuary; however, the possibility of a genuine experience of the living God will. You know what excites you about faith … now let's discover what excites **them**.

Chapter 8
Church Growth
by Teddy Kennedy

Several years ago I attended a small luncheon in Washington at which Senator Edward Kennedy was an impromptu speaker. Actually, I think he simply was introduced at the luncheon and asked to say a few words, but, as far as I was concerned, he delivered the ultimate message that day. Speaking without notes and with a weakened voice, he articulated, most powerfully, an image that still guides my thoughts. He spoke of politics, but what I heard speaks loudly to churches and to the reality so many of us are facing today.

The Republicans had just taken control of both Houses of Congress and the White House. While the nation seemed almost evenly divided, the Republicans had won it all. Acknowledging that there were many reasons for that reality, Senator Kennedy singled out one challenge that threatened to make the Democratic Party a permanent minority. He talked about the fact that, while poll after poll indicated that the majority of Americans disagree with the Republicans about many issues (abortion, gay rights, peace, education, the environment, etc.), the Republicans continue to get elected because they understand two facts:

1. The majority of Americans don't vote. Elections are decided by minorities who care enough to show up, participate and give to candidates.
2. People know where the Republicans stand on issues, and their strong stand ultimately defines the issue,

leaving Democrats to weakly react or respond. He went on to say, "Democrats are too often considered Republicans Lite, and our nation doesn't need two Republican Parties."

Regardless of whether you are a Democrat, Republican or Independent, understanding those two political realities could, and should, completely reshape how we grow our churches. Failing to understand them will lead to our eventual extinction.

Let's apply the first one to church. The Republicans built their political dynasty by appealing, relentlessly and obsessively, to what they call their base. In short, they have tailored their campaigns to turning out the conservative and Evangelical voters as sure and certain Republican votes. If we can suspend all judgment about their values, we can appreciate that this strategy has been met with great success. They have mobilized a minority of Americans to build a majority of the votes. Whether we like the outcome or not, this kind of target marketing has been most effective. While they may suffer temporary setbacks, the strength of their position should not be underestimated.

This strategy has worked, in part, because it has allowed them to tailor their message and focus it relatively tightly. They know they don't really need the support of the majority of Americans. They only need the majority of those who actually vote, and that is their target audience. Unfortunately, churches that hold inclusion as a core value seem to have great difficulty appreciating this strategy, let alone applying it. Let me offer a concrete illustration.

I recently led a church growth workshop in Oklahoma City. It was for a congregation that wanted to build their membership and attendance from approximately 75 to around 250. This was a liberal congregation of mostly lesbian and gay people. While they want to be more fully inclusive, they acknowledged that there were a number of other inclusive congregations in Oklahoma City and that their unique offering was their unconditional and even aggressive inclusion of gay and lesbian people. We spent a few minutes listing all the reasons why lesbian, gay, bisexual and transgender people might not attend their church. When the list was fairly comprehensive, I asked them what percentage of the community would be excluded because of at least one of the reasons on the list. The highest guess we got was that probably 50 percent of the LGBT community were not candidates to attend their church. With that in mind, we did a brief calculation:

- Population of the city: 530,000
- Population of urban area: 1.3 million
- LGBT population (assume 5%): 26,500/65,000
- Assume one percent of LGBT people might attend your church: 265/650

What I suggested was that they could write off as much as 99 percent of the LGBT community that lived within the city and 99.6 percent of the community in the metropolitan area, and could still easily reach their goals.

That was a great realization for them. It was much harder to recognize that, to reach their goal, they would need to write off 99 percent of the community. While that might be a bit extreme, my point was that an attempt to reach 100 percent of the community would doom their efforts to mediocrity. Perhaps it was this principle that Jesus had in mind when he addressed the church of Laodacia in the third chapter of the book of Revelation:

> *I know your works; you are neither cold nor hot.*
> *So because you are lukewarm, and neither cold nor*
> *hot, I will spit you out of my mouth.*

Jesus had no stomach for the lukewarm, and modern marketers would agree that few Americans find it very appealing today.

Our churches cannot reach everyone, but we don't need to in order to thrive. There are many churches who can reach those that we cannot. We must decide who it is we are best able to include in the family and target our efforts toward them. I repeatedly say to lay leaders who are recruiting volunteers or sponsoring events, "The least effective appeal is, 'Ya'll come.'" Time and again, however, that seems to be how we spend our marketing efforts and dollars. General invitations targeting everyone are ineffective. That is why a friend inviting a friend remains the number one reason people select new churches. Our invitations must be as personalized and targeted as possible. None of our buildings could accommodate everyone, and trying to appeal to everyone will ensure that we won't need to accommodate anyone more than those we already have.

According to the Pew Research Center, 19 percent of Americans identify themselves as liberal, 39 percent as conservative, the rest as moderate. It is quite possible that many of our particular churches will be writing off the conservative 39 percent of the population because conservatives would not be attracted to our core value of inclusion. We may also be too progressive for at least half of the moderates. However, it is an inevitable choice we must make. In fact, you have already made it. If you use gender-balanced language, encourage people to recycle, advocate for peace, support equal rights for lesbians and gays, or even women, you have already decided that your church will not be appealing to about half of the population. If you don't give an invitation to be saved, believe that homosexuality and abortion are sins, sing hymns about the blood of Jesus, you have made a choice about who will not be attending your church.

Our churches will not, and cannot, appeal to all people. Taking pro-war stands, singing nationalistic hymns, and excluding women from full leadership are also choices about the type of congregation we might attract. The problem is not the market choice we make; the problem is most churches seem completely unaware that they have already made one. Our "Ya'll Come" marketing approach pretends that everyone could find a home in our pews. That is simply not true, and, if it is, we have so compromised or hidden our core values that absolutely no one is moved or motivated.

Like the Republican Party, we don't need to appeal to everyone; we don't even need to appeal to the majority. What we must do is discover who it is that our message and ministry would appeal to and target our outreach to that group. Then, we need to fail, fail and fail again to reach them. What we have discovered is that many more of our marketing attempts fail than succeed. That shouldn't surprise us since few churches have the financial resources to do market analysis, test marketing and mass marketing. Still, it might be some comfort to know that even major corporations with marketing departments larger than our membership produce material that fails much more often than it succeeds. The one principle most marketers caution us to remember is that someone must encounter our name/identity seven times before it really has an impact. You must be prepared to fail and then try again and again.

Actually, what we have discovered is that much of our effort to reach our "target audience" succeeds more than we know. Our tendency is to send out a postcard or take out an ad and then count the number of new visitors who show up. The truth is few people are sitting around without plans for Sunday just waiting for your postcard to arrive. It may take several weeks before they have a chance to respond, and by then they will have forgotten and will need another reminder and then another. More likely, the advertisement will have planted a seed that will bear fruit on the day a friend or neighbor invites them to your church or perhaps the next time there is a crisis in their life or in our nation. On the Sunday after the tragedy of September 11, 2001 we got a true count of how effective our advertising had been when so many first-time visitors attended our church that we had to turn them away because there was not room in the building.

Beyond identifying our most likely and logical market, and targeting our outreach efforts to them, Senator Kennedy also made a second point. He told us that the country didn't need a second Republican party and that it was a mistake for the Democrats to seek to be "Republican lite." That is an important lesson for many churches, and even denominations, to learn. His remark struck me so hard because it reminded me of a lesson I had once known, but had almost forgotten.

I worked my way through college and seminary by serving as a student pastor of rural United Methodist churches. Each of the three appointments I served experienced growth, and two of them experienced significant growth. In an Evangelism class at Candler School of Theology at Emory University I created a bit of controversy by advocating that part of the reason for the decline in membership in the United Methodist Church was that few of the small towns in which I had lived really needed another Southern Baptist church, but most of my Methodist colleagues seemed to think that being more Baptist was the key to them someday becoming Bishops. In other words, we Methodists had forgotten our distinguishing gifts and, instead, were working in most communities to succeed at being "Southern Baptists Lite."

In the rural south, in almost every community, First Baptist was on one corner, and First Methodist was on the other. In the majority of small towns in the 1970s, 80s and 90s the Baptist church drew bigger crowds than the Methodist. Hence, the logic seemed to be to move more closely to the Baptists theologically and socially. Now, of course, the Southern Baptists are experiencing declines in many places, and the Methodists are discovering they abandoned their unique identity and imitated the wrong model.

The starkest illustration of this, of course, is the way the Methodist church has dealt with the ordination of homosexuals. They have violated their own basic polity and have reaped terrible division. They forgot their own history. The Anglican Church in many parts of the world is still divided over the ordination of women. By the time the Episcopal Church in America finally ordained women as priests the Methodists had been doing it for decades. By the time the Episcopal Church got around to consecrating a woman as Bishop the first woman Bishop in the Methodist Church was retired. The Methodists made the transition in this area so much earlier and more smoothly than the Episcopalians because of their polity. On every other issue concerning ordination the regional body known as the Annual Conference decides who will and will not be ordained. Even if one regarded homosexuality as a sin, why would a denomination single out this particular "sin" for church-wide exclusion? They choose to single out that one issue and violate their own polity, and they have reaped chaos and division. This has been entirely because the southern representatives of the United Methodist Church believed that, in order to compete, they had to be as aggressively socially conservative as the Baptists on the other corner.

The decline of the Methodist Church cannot be halted by them seeking to become Baptist Lite. Ironically, we live in a day when many of the core values of historic Methodism are exactly what our world most needs. In an age when people are searching for tolerance and valuing diversity, the Methodist doctrine of pluralism could serve it well. However their very public exclusion of LGBT people from full membership has left the public with little doubt about what Methodists really believe about God's inclusive love.

In 2005, the General Synod of the United Church of Christ took a very public stand supporting same-gender marriage. It seemed a logical progression for the denomination that ordained an openly gay person in 1972. In 2006, the Cathedral of Hope, known as "the largest gay church in the world" joined the United Church of Christ. The addition of our single congregation offset the membership losses that came from churches that withdrew over the "gay marriage issue." That reality can become a parable for the future I hope.

By willingly, even willfully, affirming its identity as a progressive and inclusive church, the United Church of Christ has created an identity that is unique and distinctive. It is true that conservative and fundamentalist Christians will not beat a path to our doors; it is possible, however, that their children and grandchildren will. They will not come because we are Baptist/Methodist/Presbyterian Lite; they will come because our values are congruent with theirs. While the gay issue should be a peripheral one in church polity, it has become a visible symbol of the true theology of churches. College students and 20/30-year-olds all have openly gay or lesbian friends or relatives. They will rightly make their choice of churches on the basis of how welcome their friends would be.

What should have been an incidental issue has created a divide that will be increasingly difficult to compromise. Because this issue is controversial, it will be greatly tempting to be quietly welcoming but not to make a big issue of it. That approach, however, may sacrifice our most powerful marketing tool. In his book *Hijacking Jesus*, Dan Wakefield observes:

*Christianity in the country has become almost
synonymous with right-wing fanaticism,
conservative politics, and—courtesy of Mel
Gibson—a brutally sadistic version of religious
experience. Millions of Christians like me are
appalled by this distortion of faith, which only three
decades ago stood for peace, equality, healing, and
compassion for society's outcasts—the issues that
comprised the ministry of Jesus. When I say "I'm
a Christian," I feel the need to explain myself: I'm
not one of "them," the ones who fit the image of the
faith you see in the headlines now.*

The liberal church has been in decline for some time
but not because it is liberal. If anything, it is because it was not
aggressively liberal enough to provide a social alternative.
We intellectualized the faith, homogenized worship and
soft-pedaled our core values. Soon it became true that the
only thing people got out of church was community. They
felt the church becoming increasingly irrelevant not because
we had nothing to say, but because we kept saying it so softly
or tentatively that they only thought we had nothing to say.

We became so afraid of offending someone that we
failed to challenge anyone. We are so terrified that someone
will leave that we never did anything to attract anyone new.
Again and again, I have tried to communicate one truth
about what I believe caused the Cathedral of Hope to grow
in one of the most conservative cities in America: We didn't
try to match or adapt to the conservativism of our culture.
We did not compromise or cover up our progressive values.
When he was Governor of Texas, George W. Bush cursed me
by name to a reporter because our church kept confronting
the values by which he was leading our state. While the
overwhelming majority of Texans agreed with him and
disagreed with us, God didn't call us to minister to the major-

ity. We spoke the values of Jesus as we understood them, and, though we were out of step with the majority, we were radically attractive to the minority who filled our sanctuary every Sunday.

Although I have said it before, please take seriously this lesson: Your church, like ours, needs to rediscover the kind of passion that characterizes the fundamentalist and evangelical churches in America. They know how to appeal to the hearts and passion of their congregations. Their worship is filled with fervor and excitement. They care deeply and passionately about the values they espouse. Shouldn't liberals be just as passionate about the core values of our faith? I believe it is not only safe to be fanatically devoted to certain values, but it is also necessary. Let us never be timid in our commitment to values like compassion, inclusion, justice and peace.

Since we began with a lesson in church growth from a Democrat, perhaps I should pause to quote one of the godfathers of the modern Republican Party. Barry Goldwater said, "Extremism in the defense of liberty is no vice. Moderation in the pursuit of justice is no virtue." In our context I believe God is calling us to be extremists in defense of the major core values of our faith. It is no virtue for us to be moderates in pursuit of establishing the realm of God where those virtues are our guiding principles.

By seeking to combine in equal parts the intellectual rigor of the liberal church, which values the questions, with the passion and devotion of the conservative church, the Cathedral of Hope has found a formula for growing a progressive church even in a conservative culture. We are as profoundly devoted to "saving" those "lost souls" from the hell of shame, estrangement, poverty, loneliness or hopelessness as any fundamentalist church is to saving the lost from the eternal fires of their understanding of hell. We approach our ministry with no less passion or enthusiasm.

The liberal, progressive and moderate church must learn to speak to people's hearts as effectively as we appeal to their minds. We clearly care, but who would know? In the introduction to his book *The Soul of Politics*, Jim Wallis writes:

> *The world isn't working. Things are unraveling, and most of us know it. Tonight, the urban children of the world's only remaining superpower will go to bed to the sound of gunfire. Bonds of family and community are fraying. Our most basic virtues of civility, responsibility, justice, and integrity seem to be collapsing. We appear to be losing the ethics derived from personal commitment, social purpose, and spiritual meaning. The triumph of materialism is hardly questioned now, in any part of our society. Both domestically and globally, we are divided along the lines of race, ethnicity, class, gender, religion, culture and tribe. Environmental degradation and resource scarcity threaten to explode our divisions into a world of perpetual conflict.*

He wrote those words well over a decade and a half ago, and it seems now that it may have been an optimistic assessment. Our congregations know what is happening in the world around them. What they don't know is what to do about it, what their faith says about it, and what their pastor thinks about it.

Our pews will remain more empty than filled unless we can find our prophetic voice and speak clearly and passionately to the multiple crises of our day. We are not required to have all the answers, but, as community leaders, we must at least give voice to the questions and reveal that we are struggling together to find a way. We are required by our faith to offer a word of hope so convincingly that, even in the midst of a world in despair, the realm of God might break through. Our faith speaks not of escapist optimism, but of God's word of life spoken in a land of crosses and tombs.

We must courageously accept our mantle as prophets of God and call people of faith to transformed values and lifestyles. If we refuse, we will be relegated to be the priests who offer last rites to our churches and, perhaps, to the faith we love so dearly. Millions of Americans do not wish to be a member of the civil Christianity that has come to power in this country. They are desperate for you to articulate for them an alternative.

Chapter 9
Thriving Churches

"Failure to thrive" is a medical term that denotes poor weight gain and physical growth failure over an extended period of time in infancy. Is it possible that this term can be applied to churches?

Like humans, churches that thrive do not all do so in the same way or at the same rate. Vital, healthy, thriving congregations come in many shapes, sizes and forms. A small congregation in a declining rural community that serves as a connecting force as the area transitions may be thriving as well as a suburban church that is continuously faced with space challenges. Some of the most vibrant congregations in America are located in the decaying inner-city where they meet the needs of the poor, homeless, hungry or afraid. There are congregations that have chosen the less-traveled road that they assume, like Jesus, will lead to their ultimate death, but they have chosen it because they are meeting a need and serving a desperate community.

Thriving churches, like thriving humans, all share a number of characteristics in common.

Vitality

Thriving babies are busy babies. They sleep soundly, but when they wake they are consumed by activities appropriate to their developmental stage. So, too, with thriving churches. There is a palpable energy, vitality and strength. The

Cathedral of Hope's worship is very liturgical, but it is also very energetic. There is always a loud buzz before the service as community takes place all over the sanctuary. During the course of our worship we will laugh, sometimes raucously; we will weep so openly that placed in each pew are small boxes of Kleenex; we will applaud vigorously—sometimes the announcements, sometimes the music, sometimes even the sermons. A writer for "D Magazine" who experienced our service with the overflow crowd in the sanctuary wrote, "They do worship with a capital 'W'." Even a stranger is aware when she or he has encountered a thriving church.

That can take many forms. In one of the most secular regions of the country there is a thriving congregation of mostly youth and college students that gathers each night in a gothic building to sing chants and sit in silence. The community of Taizé has certainly provided a model for vital alternative worship. I was recently honored to be the guest preacher at the Metropolitan Community Church of the Rockies in Denver, Colorado. I was surprised when their pastor told me I didn't need to bring vestments or, for that matter, a clerical collar or tie. Each Sunday, they pack a very traditional building that was once occupied by a United Methodist Church that died. They have taken out the organ and use the space with a band and multimedia screens. The service is filled with energy and with people—a group of people that the church seldom attracts in most cities.

While I believe that vital worship is the heart of a thriving church, I must confess that there are congregations who do it in other ways. Some churches pour their best resources into small groups. The "cell and celebration" model of church became quite popular in the 1990s, and it has proven effective in a culture in which extended family is a memory and authentic community a rarity. Other churches have focused their energies on serving the poor and those in need. There are a few churches that became centers for the arts, or distinguished themselves by their children's programs, or, perhaps, their programs for seniors.

The point is that a vital church is energetic and passionate about what it does well. No church can do all things well, but every thriving church has a ministry or two that it wants to share with everyone.

A baby takes hold of your finger and will not let go. "What a strong grip she has," you may say. So, too, thriving churches have a strong grip on the reality of their situation. They know their future, as well as their past. They have assessed their strengths and decided how to best utilize them in contributing to God's realm coming on earth as it is in heaven.

Healthy DNA

Thriving babies are genetically healthy. So, too, healthy, vital faith communities pay attention to their DNA. In their book *Cracking Your Congregation's Code: Mapping Your Spiritual DNA to Create Your Future*, Robert Norton and Richard Southern write:

> *There's more to your congregation than meets the eye. Just as the human organism inherits certain genetic traits, characteristics, and dispositions that in combination make up the whole person, so your congregation has a complex inheritance. Many factors, including denominational, liturgical, and cultural inheritance, go into making it what it is. Author Ken Wilber says that "to understand the whole, it is necessary to understand the parts. To understand the parts, it is necessary to understand the whole."*

Thomas Bandy is the person who first introduced me to the idea of churches having their own DNA and the importance of each congregation discerning just what theirs really is. Bandy identifies three major areas in the life of a church and 11 sub-systems of congregational life. These are as follows:

- Foundational
    o Genetic Code: the identity of the church
    o Core Leadership: the seriousness for mission in the church
    o Organization: the structure of the church for mission
- Functional
    o Changing Lives: how people experience God in the church
    o Growing Christians: how people grow in relationship to Jesus
    o Discerning Call: how people discover their place in God's plan
    o Equipping Disciples: how people are trained for ministries
    o Deploying Servants: how people are sent and supported in the world
- Formal
    o Property: the location, facility and technology
    o Finance: stewardship, budget and debt-management
    o Communication: information, marketing and advertising

As a consultant, Bandy has a series of questions in relation to each of the 11 sub-systems. He also asks for: 1) community demographic data, 2) a leadership readiness survey completed by the staff and church board and 3) a church stress test completed by the worshipping congregation, staff and church board. The differences in perception can be revealing. The gaps in the data can be significant indicators. He notes that thriving churches are always looking for extra help. This is a post-modern approach. The modern approach assumes if you are healthy you do not need help. Coaching help—not fix-it help—is the post-modern approach. Thriving churches look for ways to connect with other churches, denominational programs and/or para-church organizations in a way that supports continued learning and development.

He talks about ministry mapping not strategic planning. The strategic planning that he says is dying is long distance, linear, assumes a uniform context, emphasizes technicians, property and programs, and has a chain of command. Mission mapping is micro-macro in approach, explorational, opportunistic, based on the DNA of the organization and done in teams. According to Bandy, effective teams have a mission attitude, a work ethic, a variable plan and a winning faith. Worship reinforces the congregational DNA.

This synopsis of his work doesn't do justice to the insights he offers. Perhaps the greatest contribution that he and his colleague Bill Easum make is to challenge us to think of our congregations in new ways. The healthcare of a non-thriving infant is quite different if the challenge is genetic rather than nutritional. So, too, with our churches.

Relational

Numerous studies have been done that connect an infant's failure to thrive with touch deprivation. Children in Russian or Eastern-block countries during the Cold War often displayed symptoms of marasmus, a severe protein-energy malnutrition characterized by calorie deficiency and energy deficiency, even though they were well fed and kept in a sterile environment. It was later discovered that their disease was rooted totally in the fact that infants need affection and physical touch almost as much as they need nutrition.

This seems an important lesson for liberal and progressive churches to learn. People need to be touched as much as they need to be informed. Our worship, sermons and programs should be shaped to touch people and connect them to God, and one another, as much as to educate them and inform them about God. In fact, we live in a day when people hunger much more for an encounter with God than they do for information about God. Our theological education serves us only in as much as it equips us to help our congregants join hands with one another, the world and the Ultimate.

Dr. Leonard Sweet, talking about the shift from a modern to post-modern world on his website, www.leonardsweet.com, says, "Someday I will hold up my Bible before a congregation, shake it, and yell at the top of my lungs, 'This is not a book about propositions and programs and principles. This is a book about relationships.'"

He uses the acronym EPIC to describe how the church must function in a post-modern world. EPIC stands for Experiential, Participatory, Image rich and Connected. In his book *Postmodern Pilgrims,* Dr. Sweet makes a strong case for the shifts that our churches must make if we are going to be relevant to the lives of those growing up on Starbucks and E-Bay.

An infant will not thrive no matter how many times a parent tells them they love them. Babies must be touched and so must our congregations. Babies must be nourished and have their needs met and so must our congregations. This is not to say that we need to treat church members like babies; it simply is to say that we must treat them like humans—humans living in the 21st century. They are busy and often hurting people who don't have time to participate in activities that do not add value to their lives. Among the deepest needs modern Americans have are community, connection and contact with one another and, we believe, with God. This is exactly what the church has to offer. So, why aren't our churches thriving? In part, it is because we are still functioning within a 20th century paradigm. The seminaries most of us attended were 19th century institutions that struggled to join the modern world. Unfortunately, the shift had been made to a post-modern reality. As Dr. Lyle Schaller is fond of saying, "If we wake up tomorrow and it is 1950 our churches are ready."

Please do not hear this as advocating that the only way the church can thrive is to discard or disregard the needs of older generations. The truth is, though, as our older members face the end of their lives they would much rather have a hand to hold than theology to learn. Unlike their own parents and grandparents, this generation of seniors is the first in history to face the ends of their lives NOT surrounded by extended family members. Their children, grandchildren, nieces and nephews are scattered to the four winds. The church has the perfect opportunity to be their extended family and to truly be there for them. We must recognize this connectional need and meet it in such a way that the succeeding generations will recognize that church is still the place where they can belong from birth to death.

During the AIDS crisis the Cathedral of Hope suffered greatly. Leader after leader was stricken and died. Six of the 10 people who served on the committee that called me to be their pastor were dead before I celebrated my seventh anniversary. The church itself easily could have died. Many predominantly LGBT churches did. However, our congregation rose up to care for the sick and dying so aggressively that every funeral and memorial became an evangelism event. People would rise to talk about the deceased, but, inevitably, they also would talk about the members of our congregation who had been with him until the end. They would bear witness to the caring grace of this place called hope, and people at the service who hadn't been inside a church in years decided to give it another try. The year when we read more than 180 names on All Saints Sunday, we also received more than 300 new members.

Nourishment

Infants, of course, need adequate nourishment in order to thrive. The Church Vitality program of the United Church of Christ suggests that one of the "Vital Signs" is nurturing faith. They offer an extensive list of educational programs for use in our congregations at www.uccvitality.org/resources. These resources are great, because there is a deep spiritual hunger in this country for spiritual guidance and enlightenment. Notice, I did not say that there was a great need for information. What can we tell our congregations that they cannot learn in seconds by typing a few words into Google? In a recent class I taught on the history of the UCC, I found the information more concisely presented on Wikipedia than in any of the incredibly well written UCC books that I own. More information is really not what most people need.

Like me, you probably grew up going to Sunday School. There, you probably learned things such as how many books there were in the Bible and the names of the four Gospels. There have been a number of articles about the appalling biblical illiteracy that exists in our world today. Bill McKibben wrote a great article for "Harper's" magazine entitled "The Christian Paradox" in which he observed:

Only 40 percent of Americans can name more than four of the Ten Commandments, and a scant half can cite any of the four authors of the Gospels. ... This failure to recall the specifics of our Christian heritage may be further evidence of our nation's educational decline, but it probably doesn't matter all that much in spiritual or political terms. Here is a statistic that does matter: Three quarters of Americans believe the Bible teaches that "God helps those who help themselves." That is, three out of four Americans believe that this uber-American idea, a notion at the core of our current individualist politics and culture, which was in fact uttered by Ben Franklin, actually appears in Holy Scripture. The thing is, not only is Franklin's wisdom not biblical; it's counter-biblical. Few ideas could be further from the gospel message, with its radical summons to love of neighbor. On this essential matter, most Americans—most American Christians—are simply wrong, as if 75 percent of American scientists believed that Newton proved gravity causes apples to fly up.

Asking Christians what Christ taught isn't a trick. When we say we are a Christian nation—and, overwhelmingly, we do—it means something. People who go to church absorb lessons there and make real decisions based on those lessons; increasingly, these lessons inform their politics. (One poll found that 11 percent of U.S. churchgoers were urged by their clergy to vote in a particular way in the 2004 election, up from 6 percent in 2000.) When George Bush says that Jesus Christ is his favorite philosopher, he may or may not be sincere, but he is reflecting the sincere beliefs of the vast majority of Americans.

It is important that we educate people to carry on the faith. However, I have come to believe that people know what is important to them, what helps them get through each day, what improves their life, and what might be helpful to them or their families. The average American's appalling religious education is testimony to the fact that we have not convinced them that what we have to offer can help their daily life and nourish their souls.

My life partner since 1980, Bill, is a certified wine educator. There are a variety of ways to teach people more about wine, and there are a number of reasons why wine classes are so popular these days. One, of course, is that people enjoy learning. If that was the primary motivation, though, he would be out of business pretty fast. Most people who take these classes want to know more about wine so they won't be embarrassed when ordering wine in a restaurant or by serving the "wrong wine" for dinner. Bill recognized early on that most of his students didn't really want to know the various regions where certain grapes were grown or the soil acidity or climate contrasts that produce certain varietals. He had to know all of these things because he was a professional. He also had to learn them to graduate. Now, his library is full of books he never uses, and his head is full of information that no one really cares about. He could impose this information on his classes because he finds it fascinating or because he thinks it is important. Ultimately, though, his philosophy is to let people taste wines paired with the various foods they might order or serve so that they will know what wine enhances their dining experience. Let those who have ears hear …

Ultimately, we must offer our members the information that will enhance their spiritual lives. We must help them learn spiritual principles for living their lives. When we do this they will come to value the source of this information: the church, the Bible, theology, etc. I am often asked by members which version of the Bible they should buy. It is a question that warms any pastor's heart because it signifies a spiritual hunger. I have taken to suggesting that rather than starting with a 2,000-year-old writing, perhaps they might read a couple of books *about* the Bible. I have discovered that people who first read, for example, Marcus Borg's *Reading the Bible Again for the First Time* are far more likely to make it out of Genesis chapter one.

Church thrives in a variety of ways. I probably have carried the analogy of infants thriving too far already, but let me offer one last parallel. A thriving infant brings beauty to the whole world. None of us are so cynical that we can resist smiling back into the face of a happy, healthy cooing baby. Having been a pastor for decades to a community that sees the church as the enemy of its civil rights and happiness, I am very conscious of how the community responds to our churches. Do they see us as an asset to the common life of the neighborhood, town or city where we are located? Is it a place to which they would send their children, take their friends, suggest to new neighbors? Do they think we are a thriving, vibrant, relevant place where people go to experience God and join community? Or do they see us as a place where something happens on Sunday mornings, but they haven't a clue what? Worse yet, maybe they don't even see us at all because we are so irrelevant to their lives. Even in a crisis, it would never cross their minds to cross our thresholds. There are lots of ways for a church to thrive, but I think that those that don't want to find at least one way ought to turn their facility into a theater or community center. At least, then, someone's needs are being met there.

Chapter 10
A Metanoia Church

One of my closest friends has had a very successful business career. He has risen to the top but has used a unique strategy. Unlike most folks who move from success to success, he has specialized in what he calls "turn-arounds." He enjoys taking a failing or underperforming company and helping it to turn around and become successful.

As Christians, we ought to be the ultimate turn-around specialists. The Greek word "metanoia" occurs in the Bible dozens of times. It is generally translated "repent." Among us liberal-types the concept of repentance often has gotten a bad rap. Of course, that, in large part, is because some of our fellow Christians have insisted on screaming it at us, often about things that we didn't really think needed changing, like sexual orientation or progressive social values. Still, even the most liberal of us understand that the Biblical concept of repentance is actually **good** news. The idea that the God who created us believes we are capable of a change in the direction of our lives should encourage us and give us hope. If that is true about our lives, then why not our churches?

While metanoia is a multifaceted word, its basic meaning is, "To change direction." If unprofitable companies can be turned around, certainly churches or ministries that are not thriving can as well. I must confess that I, on occasion, have been asked to consult with a church that was declining and facing the end of its life and said to myself, "Saving that church is probably impossible." That is the kind of statement that can really only be made confidently by an atheist. If Easter has any meaning at all in our lives it is that God is the God of alternative endings.

So, can every situation be turned around? Our faith must say, "Yes, it is always possible." However, like humans and almost every human creation, churches have natural life cycles, and it may be that the end of a church is the natural and appropriate occurrence with the passage of time. As painful as it is, some churches must die so that something else can be born. However, I personally believe that reality should be much rarer than it is today for progressive, liberal and mainline churches. Yes, death is the only option for some, but many simply need to find the right formula to turn around trends that, if neglected, will lead to their demise.

Turning around a loss of membership, attendance, finances and/or vitality is never easy, and this is a case of "one size fits some." Each situation is so unique it requires a unique solution to its challenges. However, my business friend suggests that there are basic principles and steps for any company that wants to turn around their losses, and I think that is true in our churches too. They, in fact, may be very similar. Let's see:

Ruthless Honesty

The first step may be the hardest because for any change of direction to occur we must be absolutely truthful about the fact that we are headed in the wrong direction. Like the old-fashioned concept of repentance, confession is a vital, though painful, stage through which we must move. If you have ever had to make a deep, soul-bearing confession of your own failures, you know just how traumatic this can be. Generally, though, our failures are not built on some major soul-rattling mistake, but are the result of a series of tiny misjudgments usually rooted in some mistaken core beliefs or self delusion.

Every time I ask a church why they believe they are not thriving, almost everyone in the room has a quick answer. Sometimes everyone has a different theory, and sometimes it is a part of the commonly held belief of that faith community: the neighborhood is changing, population is declining, not enough parking, we lost our beloved pastor, the building is such bad repair, etc. All of these reasons, and dozens more, certainly can contribute to the loss of vitality in a congregation. Yet we all can cite examples of churches that are exceptions—churches that thrive under all of these same circumstances. The tough thing is to get below those obvious and legitimate concerns until we are able to address the root causes of a congregation's inability to be one of the exceptions.

There are a number of tools that are available to do an accurate assessment of a church's circumstances, challenges and potential for vitality. This may be THE area where an outside "expert" may be of greatest service. Any of us can utilize the tools available, but it is difficult for a pastor or longtime lay leaders to deliver, frankly enough, the bad news that first must be ruthlessly faced. It feels like a betrayal, and it is good that the "betrayer" can go away soon after the diagnosis. Physicians often have to tell us bad news, but generally they don't have to live with us afterwards. Or, as John Fortunado, in his book *Embracing the Exile*, puts it, "The bad news about therapy is you **don't** die." The pain of this kind of brutal honesty won't kill a church, but it can kill a relationship with a pastor who was called to preach good news not bad.

While Elizabeth Kubler-Ross's stages of death and dying are no longer in vogue with grief counselors, they still illuminate some of the reactions our congregations have to a painful diagnosis. Denial is a natural first response, but it also can be a fatal one. Pretending it isn't there and allowing a tumor to grow until we are too weak to respond to treatment seems to symbolize the approach too many non-thriving congregations take. Frankly, we pastors must accept some responsibility for being complicit in this denial. Our friends in recovery keep trying to remind us that the very definition of crazy is *doing the same thing and expecting different results*. Yet I so often find myself unable to change course because I am doing what I know how to do and am terrified to admit that it is no longer working and that I need to learn some new skills.

Remembering Our Business

Closely linked to the first need required for turn around is the leadership again answering the late Peter Drucker's core question: "What business are you in?" The great management guru was fond of asking that question of everyone in a company, from the Board of Directors to the CEO to the shipping clerk. He often noted that, while he generally would get congruent answers to the question, he almost always would get the wrong one.

"We're in the steel business," or "We're in the hotel business." Lawyers were in the law business, and accountants in the accounting business. "No," said Drucker. "The purpose of the corporation is almost always to make new customers." This simple-sounding concept is at the core of Drucker's philosophy. In concert with Dr. Lyle Schaller, Drucker tried to remind us that the church was in the business of making disciples of Jesus. New disciples are our customers. Evangelism and discipleship remain the two core functions of the modern church today. Reach them and teach them. The methodology we use must adapt and change almost daily, but our business remains the one assigned to us by Jesus.

Yes, building community, serving the poor, worshipping God, helping the hurting, transforming society and confronting injustice are all quite legitimate functions of a vital church. However, these functions all are carried forward by disciples. We who have devoted ourselves to the way of Jesus do the work of Jesus. There is a natural order to that, and the modern progressive church often fails to prioritize the first step. It is a great thing for a child to grow up to be a physician. However, she must first be born/come into the family; then she must be trained and educated. Even after she becomes a physician, she must be properly equipped and supported by a competent, congruent community.

Evangelism, discipleship and service occur in that order. Churches that neglect the first two steps often find themselves giving their life for Christ without giving birth to those who will replace them after they are gone. Many of the most ancient admonitions of the Hebrew Scriptures are rooted in the Jew's awareness that unless they propagated they would not survive. While the rules are outdated, that principle is not. Our pews are no longer filled by our biological children, and we must borrow a page from the evangelical churches in America if we are to fill them again. How did evangelism and growth become so derided in progressive circles? If we have found our faith to be a gift, and if we believe that the values we have to offer are good, true and transformative, we ought to be about sharing them. Evangelism is not about converting people so they won't go to hell as much as it is about liberating people from the hells in which they find themselves trapped: consumerism, purposelessness, isolation, greed, shame, fear, alienation, etc. If we have any good news for them then our first business is to offer it.

I once had to turn down a $250,000 gift. The donor wanted to endow a secular scholarship fund that the Church would administer. After listening to his expectations, it was easy for me to say, "That is a great idea and a wonderfully generous thing to do, but that is not the business we are in. Let me put you in touch with someone who would be better equipped to do what you need." In the same way, after many successful years of helping people, our church had to shut down its counseling center. It was a thriving concern, but, when we looked closely at the services we were providing, we realized that what had originally been a ministry had evolved into a business. When we began the program there were few counselors to serve the lesbian and gay community, and even fewer to assist people living with AIDS. Two decades later that was no longer the case. We actually were competing with other organizations, and even businesses, to provide services that were not our specialty. We still provide spiritual and pastoral counseling, but we no longer employ 28 therapists to provide clinical psychotherapy. Like the scholarships, therapy is a very good thing; it just is not **our** thing.

It is easy to get distracted and forget what business we are in, but, as Peter Drucker observed, it also is easy to spend all of our time and resources running a machine and forget what the machine was designed to produce. All too often, I have seen churches and organizations that produce just enough resources to run the church or organization, but not enough to fulfill their purpose. That is like maintaining a machine that generates only enough energy to run the machine. No matter how beautiful or well run the machine may be, it ultimately is worthless because it serves no greater purpose than itself.

• • •

High Failure Rate

ESPN should not exist today. It does because "Sports Illustrated" forgot what business it was in. The people at "Sports Illustrated," which was launched in 1964, came to believe that they were in the business of publishing magazines. If they had remembered that their true business was providing the public with information and entertainment about sports, they would have continued to find new ways to do that. Since they did not, ESPN was born in 1979 and today has a customer base and income stream that dwarfs the magazine, which today is known almost as much for its swim suit coverage as its sports coverage.

Renewing the vitality of a church requires us to remember what business we are in and then to get out of our boxes in terms of how we do that business. What that means is that we must dare to see new visions, dream new dreams, and try new things. The key to that is we must be free from our fear of failure.

While many people believe the Cathedral of Hope's growth was the result of my success rate, the truth of the matter is it was much more dependent on my failure rate. I simply tried more things that failed than most of my peers. This is a great testimony, not to me, but to the lay people with whom I have had the privilege to work. The Board of Directors and I both knew we were doing something that had never been tried before; therefore we were going to have to try a lot of things that had never been tried before to reach our goal. We wanted to include large numbers of mostly lesbian and gay people in an institution that had historically excluded and even abused them. We also wanted to build a progressive, inclusive and theologically-liberal congregation in one of the most conservative cities in America.

Early on, we discovered that just because someone might be lesbian or gay does not mean they are progressive. In fact, as we considered the dynamics, we acknowledged that our goals would probably be met if we simply refurbished the evangelical message and ministry with which most of our "customers" had grown up. Those who grew up in more progressive faith traditions often simply walked away when they heard that, as the Methodists say, "Homosexuality is incompatible with the Christian teachings." However, those who grew up in more conservative and fear-based traditions were often the ones who clung to their faith even while acknowledging their sexual orientations. In other words, our largest market was lesbian, gay, bisexual and transgender people who were still mostly fundamentalist or, at least, evangelicals in fear of hell. One of our church leaders observed early on in our efforts to build a progressive church in Dallas, "This is like we are trying to build a market for a Sushi restaurant in Italy."

Trying things that didn't work was the only tool we had. We read all the books and tried repeatedly to engage various consultants. No purpose would be served by me providing you the names of the churches, clergy or consultants who refused to work with us. This rejection is one of the reasons we so love Dr. Lyle Schaller, who was unique in his willingness to help and his continued friendship. By and large, though, we were left to find our way largely by trial and error. That can only be done well in a safe place. With very few exceptions, the congregation was willing to follow as leaders tried new things that often didn't work. My partners on the Board of Directors were possessed of an entrepreneurial spirit and never made me afraid that my many failures might lead to them losing confidence in me. We've had some rather spectacular failures, too, but, along the way, we have known enough success to build a historically large, vital and growing liberal church in a most unlikely setting.

I suppose I also should pause to confess the fact

that, in addition to finding ways to attract record numbers of new people, I probably also hold the record for running off the most people. While many were estranged through mistakes I made, failed relationships, and my own deeply flawed humanity, a significant number left the church because we needed them to. In our more crass moments, clergy are prone to joke that our churches are just a couple of funerals away from revival, and there is more than a sliver of truth in that. When I arrived in Dallas and became clear of what the congregation's vision was for the church I knew that to achieve their goals would require a redefinition of who they were as a church. They were one of the largest Metropolitan Community Churches in the country at that time with almost 300 members. However, that was the challenge. The congregation wanted to be a very large church: "Large enough to change the way lesbian and gay people think about God and large enough to change how the world thinks about lesbian and gay people." Well, given that assignment, the standard MCC formula wasn't going to work, because no MCC had ever grown much beyond the size that congregation was in 1987. That remains true today.

One of the irresistible realities of life is that death is required to make way for birth. While everyone wishes it were different, there really is no escaping this truth, nor has anyone found a real alternative. In order for our congregation to give birth to something that had never existed before—an LGBT mega-church—who we had been would have to die. Naturally, there were those who were strongly attached to the existing values, styles and identity. As the leadership laid out a new course, the biggest unanswered question was if people would resist changing the church they had known and loved, participate in the transformation, or simply leave. Ultimately, we discovered that those who worked for change far outnumbered those who resisted it. That is usually the case when changes are sensitively made and adequately explained. However, many churches have learned the hard way that a small group, or even a single influential resistor, can derail critically needed changes. We discovered that one of the greatest gifts we received during that time was the large number of people who simply left.

Let me say that these were not bad people. Most were folks who decided that the church they needed and wanted was different from the church we were becoming. That certainly was fair. It was a testament to the authenticity of their faith that they did not insist that the church be what they personally wanted/needed it to be, but, rather, left to find a church that better met their needs. Still, the departures were painful, and a congregation already deeply in grief suffered further. As an antidote, we brought new members into the church with a great sense of joy and celebration. We expanded the ritual, had parties and celebrations, took them into the family in large groups, and encouraged them to invite family and friends to attend with them. The impression the average congregant got during that two-year span was that the church was growing rapidly. While they might have disagreed with some of the changes, they didn't question the results and were therefore much more willing to offer grace. Statistically, however, the truth was, after two years of my leadership, the church was only slightly larger than when I arrived. We had taken in many new members but I had alienated more than a few.

Had that reality continued the results would have been disastrous. At one point another church was began in town that largely was made up of former members. This church was, and is, strongly evangelical in theology and worship and has been led by pastors who were formerly Baptist. Since Southern Baptist is, by far, the largest denomination in Dallas, it was a natural fit for the market. That church grew quickly and is today a vital and healthy congregation of around 300 members. The formation of this church caused a great deal of fear in our leadership, but it was a wonderful gift. As our church continued to become more theologically liberal and increasingly liturgical, our sibling congregation provided a healthy and much-needed alternative. The year following their formation saw our congregation explode in growth. Although we were meeting in a wretched temporary space in an office building, we nearly doubled in size. While we grieved the loss of community with those who left, there was a liberation that we never could have anticipated. That is not because those who left were "wrong," but because we were free to answer a different call without hurting them and their needs. As painful as it was, that time was a liberating gift for us all. Although we did not see this at the time, we fortunately acted out of grace, and today can recognize the work of the Spirit who was multiplying, not dividing.

Creating a culture of grace within the church where we can take chances and make mistakes is not optional. When a body ceases to grow and change it dies. Change always is unsettling for everyone, which is why heaping doses of grace are needed. Still, finding new ways to tell the "old, old story" is critical if we are to turn around mainline churches. What originally built our churches long ago ceased to attract crowds of new disciples and young people. We do not need to change our message so much as we must change our method. Thomas Edison always believed that his rate of success was in direct portion to the height of the trash pile outside his laboratory. He said, "I am not discouraged, because every wrong attempt discarded is another step forward." He also said, "Opportunity is missed by most people because it is dressed in overalls and looks like work."

• • •

Hard Work

I have finally reached the stage in my life where I can admit that some things don't succeed because I simply did not want to work that hard. To be sure, one key to success for every leader is their willingness to do the work that is necessary. Much of that work must take place within us. In liberal circles "self care" has often become the third sacrament. We have become so afraid of burning out that we never get warmed up. Does that seem unkind and unfair? Perhaps, but I am only saying aloud what many of our lay people believe. Ministry can be a haven for the lazy, complacent and unmotivated. Too often, we simply don't want to do the hard work that will be required to renew the vitality of the church. Over the years, I have been incredibly frustrated by a number of seminary graduates who thought they deserved to be the Senior Pastor of the Cathedral of Hope, but were completely unwilling to earn the job or, better yet, build their own congregations. Lay people look at us and wonder how we can ask them to volunteer or take on additional responsibility in addition to the 40 or 50 hours their fulltime jobs require. Their resentment is that we are asking them to do what we seem unwilling to do. When pastors clock out after 40 hours we lose our moral right to ask our members to volunteer on their nights and weekends off.

Now, that paragraph was full of hyperbole. Many, if not most, of the clergy in this country are devoted women and men who give much more than 40 hours a week to their jobs. That is not, however, how we frequently are seen. Lay people often wonder what we do all day, and, frankly, I wonder that myself sometimes about my own day. Yet I sure stay busy and never seem to get all my work done. Even as a borderline workaholic, I feel guilty that I am not doing enough. The secret I repeatedly have discovered, and then repeatedly forgotten, is that I have to spend my time and energy working very hard doing the right things. Doing the right things may be more important than doing things right. What is it in my weekly schedule that **only** I can do, and, ultimately, what is it that pays the biggest dividend for the church and the Realm of God?

If life was fair the things I love to spend my time doing would be the exact things that produce the most results. In case you haven't already noticed, life isn't fair. When I was a small-town Methodist pastor, I loved visiting shut-ins and people at the hospital. It is a worthy and fulfilling ministry, but it is not one that requires me personally to do it. During the worst of the AIDS crisis at the Cathedral of Hope it became an overwhelming and devastating ministry. I was in my mid-30s, and one day I walked into two hospital rooms, side-by-side, with four young men my age who were dying. I was almost incoherent the rest of the day. The staggering weight of that forced us to recruit large teams of people and train them for this ministry. The result was that I rarely do hospital visits any more. The other result was that a large number of people grew as disciples and those who needed visiting got much better, and more frequent, service. At one point we had dozens of people in hospitals all over the city who were visited by the church every single day. Many times church members would be by their bedsides 24 hours a day.

I have no doubt that pastors work hard because they are devoted servants of Jesus and because they never would take money they didn't earn. My challenge to most pastors is to decide where your hard work will produce the most results. Anything that **you** don't have to do give away as ministry to others. Giving away the ministry doesn't give you more time to sit around and pray or watch TV or read theology or science fiction. What it can do is free you up to invest your time and energy in places with the greatest impact. Most of us are too busy now; the trouble is we too often are busy doing the wrong things.

Conclusions

The point I think is that turn-arounds are never easy. You have to be willing to work very hard, and your leaders do too. You need a small group who are willing to say, "For the next couple of years I'm willing to give this my highest priority and my best effort." You have to be willing to say that as well. It is unlikely you have an extra dozen hours a week to devote to this, so you are going to have to ruthlessly eliminate the important and do the vital. You will work harder than ever, but your focus will be doing those things that produce results—results in your own life, results in the life of your church. Here, the 80/20 principle is true: 20 percent of your work will produce 80 percent of the results of your ministry. With severely limited resources, my suggestion is that pastors and congregations in turn-around situations must focus 100 percent on the productive 20 percent. Despite what I said above, you probably can't work any harder, so you must discover how to work much smarter. Take shortcuts with the important; concentrate on the vital. Let others do what others can and you work harder on those things that will produce results:

- Vibrant worship.
- Relevant and dynamic preaching.
- Leadership training/"equipping the saints."
- Infusing disciples with the God-given vision.
- Evangelism—birthing the next generation.

You may have a different list, and your situation may require one. But make the list, and if it is not on the list don't do it. Then figure out how to do the list more effectively. Turning around must begin as a decision in the heart of those who are steering the ship.

The Cathedral of Hope only vaguely resembles the

church that elected a 33-year-old former Methodist from South Georgia as its pastor in 1987. I can't believe how much it has grown and changed. I can't believe how much I have. My biggest regret is that I didn't grow and change more, but, God willing, there is still time.

Through the late 1980s and 90s this church needed prophetic leadership because it was living in hostile territory and a plague threatened its very life. Today, the world has changed. Dallas has changed. And the type of leadership this church needs has changed. In 2005, the Cathedral of Hope elected a new Senior Pastor. The church became one of the largest in the world to be led by a woman. The Rev. Dr. Jo Hudson has brought incredible gifts, energy, passion and joy to this congregation. She is a most unique individual; one evidence that I would offer is that she asked that I remain as a part of the leadership of this congregation. Now, I feel like an elder, though I like to pretend I am still a youth.

Although I originally hired her, Jo is now my boss. That has been the easiest part of this transition. She is a dear and beloved friend. I don't mind preaching less, doing secondary services on big holidays, giving up my role leading the staff or the Board. I don't even mind giving up "my chair" on the chancel. It has been harder to sit while another does the baptisms and confirms new members. Letting go and supporting change is tough, and I've gotten to know just how tough firsthand. While I'm not always successful, I, frankly, have surprised myself by how well I've done.

Recently, I visited my parents who are now quite elderly. They have been members of that First United Methodist Church in my hometown for 35 years now. They have both served in almost every leadership role possible. That church was where I came to love and value strong liturgy and beautiful historic worship. That church has the most beautiful stained glass and the best organ in that part of the country. The Sunday I visited my parents they had to go to church early because they were ushering at the early service, which is held in the Fellowship Hall and where they sing contemporary praise songs accompanied by a band. It attracts mostly young people and college students, lasts only 45 minutes, always starts late, and sounds like organized chaos to me. Yet that is where these two old southern Methodist serve. I shook my head as they went off to church that morning, and I went to catch a plane. For a moment I just had to pause and pray that God would keep my own heart as vibrant and flexible as theirs.

That is the key to prophetic renewal for the mainline church and is my prayer for the heart of us all.

Amen.

Chapter 11
Show Me the Money

Some people might think that the phrase used for this chapter title comes from the 1996 Academy Award-winning film "Jerry McGuire." However, we in the church know the true source. Although Jesus used slightly different phrasing, he was the one who said, "Show me your treasure and I'll tell you the truth about your heart." (Matthew 6:21, Piazza paraphrase)

On any given day, I change my mind about why church leaders avoid, or at least flinch when it comes to, teaching and preaching about money. Some days I think it is because we still haven't made peace with our own money issues. Seminary sure doesn't teach you how to have a healthy relationship with the most powerful force in our society. My parents treated money a lot like sex—it was something taken care of behind closed doors and not in front of the kids. We always sensed when there was something wrong in that area, but no one ever sat me down and had a father/mother to son dollars and cents talk. Most of us learned what we knew about money "on the street" or by trial and error.

When Bill and I became a couple in 1980 money was the area of life where our values conflicted the most. We never really fought about it, but it took a lot of late night talking to uncover the roots of our values and why we dealt with money the way that we did. Fortunately, when it came to church, my family lived out of a sense of almost illogical generosity. Bill's family were dutiful Baptists, so, from day one, there was no conflict about our giving a generous proportion to the church. As our lives became more financially secure, through the years we came to realize that we could afford to give considerably more than the standard 10 percent. During the times when we struggled to make our own ends meet we managed to look up and see that much of the world around us didn't even have ends. To that another of Jesus' pithy sayings seemed to speak: "To whom much is given, much is expected." Essentially, our conscience wouldn't allow us to enjoy all we had until we felt we were doing as much as possible to help others have more.

We were the fortunate ones. Both of our families seemed to have reasonably healthy relationships with money, and we inherited this relationship. We can take no credit for that, and for many years didn't even recognize it. Through the years, in the context of both pastoral counseling and friendships, I became painfully aware that money was the source of a significant portion of conflicts in relationships. So, too, in my consulting work with churches, I have come to realize that, if a pastor has been in a church more than four years and the church is having financial conflicts or a short-fall, there is a good chance that the pastor and his/her family have personal money issues.

Once upon a time I naively assumed that all pastors and church leaders gave generously. Over the years, though, I have found that the pastors on my own staff were often the best paid and the least generous of staff leaders. In our system, the Board of Directors has the responsibility of financial oversight, but all too often they didn't assume personal responsibility.

All of this may seem like I am meddling in personal issues, however it has been a consistent truth that resolving a church's financial challenges must always begin with helping leadership resolve theirs. In some cases, pastors have missed the reality that, despite their best efforts, a congregation always knows what a pastor does or does not give. Modeling generosity is a crucial foundation for faithful stewardship, and failure to do so provides many the excuse they need to avoid their own responsibilities. Why should they sacrifice to financially advance the Realm of God if their spiritual leader does not do so? We cannot speak of stewardship with conviction unless we also speak with integrity. We cannot effectively teach that which we do not really know or truly believe.

Perhaps there is a more metaphysical reality here. There is one scripture about which I am a fundamentalist, because I am convinced it is one of the fundamental laws of the universe: "What we sow we also reap." If we who would lead are conflicted about money and not able to be live with integrity, generosity and gratitude, we seem to unconsciously sow those very seeds in the souls of our congregations. Only the generous person can speak of generosity without a catch in their throat.

The other reason that congregational leaders avoid speaking directly and effectively about money is that religious hucksters have given us all a bad reputation. Sinclair Lewis' 1927 novel "Elmer Gantry" and the 1960 movie based upon it haunt us all. More contemporaneously were the televangelists and their scandals and, now, those preachers touting the "Prosperity Gospel." Who can blame us for not wanting to be associated with any of them? And, at the risk of rubbing salt in wounds I have already inflicted, let me add that our fears of appearing to channel a televangelist are greatly magnified if our own consciences are not clear. This guilt/shame is compounded by the fact that almost every pastor's livelihood is funded by the giving of our members. Let's simply acknowledge that creates a nearly intolerable conflict of interest. Yet even that does not excuse us of our responsibility to be true to the full message of the gospel.

All of these seem to be principle reasons why we

don't do an adequate job of teaching people how to be good stewards of their resources. Let me suggest the two very basic reasons we must overcome these encumbrances and become effective spiritual leaders in this area.

First, we must do this because it is a prominent, perhaps dominant, spiritual truth taught in the Bible. We liberals are as guilty as fundamentalists of seeing what we are looking for when we read the Bible. Yet, a naïve reading of the Gospels would probably shock us in this area. Jesus talks about money, materialism, possessions and stewardship more than all other issues combined; in fact, some say more than **all** other subjects combined. Jesus didn't talk about money as a fundraising technique, but as a core principle of life. This would be a strong argument for separating our stewardship lessons from our pledge campaigns. Jesus told parables of stewardship as a matter of course in talking about how we live our lives. We who are faithful to the assigned lessons of the lectionary cannot avoid talking about money.

From John 3:16's message of God's giving, to the self-giving kenosis of Jesus in Philippians, giving is such a core message of Christianity that I would argue that only the generous can be true disciples of Jesus.

The other reason I believe it is critical that we not neglect our responsibility in this area is that nothing is more damaging to our people than the hold materialism has on our souls. **Generosity is the only antidote**.

It is the lesson Jesus tried repeatedly to teach, but the multi-billion marketing industry has not only completely drowned out that message, but has hijacked Jesus for their merchandising purposes. A few years ago when marketers at General Motors used the old Shaker tune "'Tis a Gift to be Simple" to sell one of its highest priced vehicles I knew we were in a struggle to the death for the souls of our people. As contemporary spiritual leaders, you don't need me to tell you how pervasive this disease is or the extent of its devastation. I'm sure you have quoted the statistics in your own lessons.

In his book *The Crisis in the Church: Spiritual Malaise and Fiscal Woe*, Robert Wuthnow grieves for the lack of economic and stewardship visions in the church and for its failure of spirit. He places much of the responsibility at the feet of pastors.

A decade ago Donald A. Luidens, who was then professor of sociology at Hope College in Holland, Michigan, wrote an excellent analysis of Wuthnow's work in "Christian Century":

> *Wuthnow describes the churches' "fiscal woes" in great detail. He suggests, however, that they are mere symptoms of the real issue, which "is a spiritual crisis [that] derives from the very soul of the church. The problem lies less in parishioners' pocketbooks than in their hearts and less in churches' budgets than in clergy's understanding of the needs and desires of their members' lives." Sadly, many clergy simply don't understand that the core problem is a "spiritual malaise." The carrier of that disease is middle-class culture. The middle-class ethos, the cultural ecology within which the church exists, is replete with themes that have stifled parishioners' spirit. As members of the middle class themselves, clergy are blind to the cultural motifs that threaten their parishioners' well-being and the churches' survival.*

There is a grave danger in the fact that we are inevitably infected by the same disease that afflicts the overwhelming majority of our congregations, and we, therefore, don't feel the sense of urgency to offer a cure. Like most middle-class people, we, too, feel overwhelmed by demands. At work, at leisure or at home, people can barely contend with all that is expected of them. From the proverbial "soccer moms," to the overextended professionals and managers, to blue- and white-collar workers facing the abyss of unemployment, middle-class Americans are riven by angst over what lies before them and by guilt over what they have left undone.

Wuthnow goes on describing their dilemma and ours:

> *They can't even talk about their predicament, since financial matters are considered private, not to be spoken of even to one's pastor or fellow parishioners. Christians lack an effective vocabulary for discussing with each other the economic and financial pressures on their lives. Lacking a theological framework, clergy too easily lapse into the saccharin reassurances of a gospel of happiness, which stresses health and wealth and simplistically equates faithful living with economic success and personal happiness. Or they proclaim a message of passive dependence—"God will provide"—which fosters complacency and inaction. Neither the gospel of happiness nor the gospel of dependence offers practical hope.*

Church leaders' ignorance and anxieties about the mechanics of the economy confound these problems. Wuthnow points out that many clergy are highly suspicious of the "secular" world of work. To the many who have never been employed outside the church, the world of secular employment is foreign, perhaps hostile, territory. Second-career pastors have generally felt themselves "called out" of the secular workforce. Consequently, they too often do not see the work environment in positive theological terms. Clergy suspicions of the work world have been reinforced by their counseling of parishioners who have been wounded by overwork, unemployment, absentee parenthood or other malignancies related to work.

Wuthnow points out that the vast majority of Americans love their jobs and find their identity inextricably wrapped up in them. Their occupation is where their heart finds its home, a place of considerable reward and fulfillment—a place begging for theological definition. Most people are so tied to their occupations that their fear of losing their jobs has as much to do with its threat to their identities as with the loss of income. Because clergy do not fully recognize this reality, Wuthnow argues, they do not realize the importance of thinking theologically about work. Wuthnow wants the church to reclaim the concept of vocation as it applies to the work life of each Christian. Since clergy regularly refer to their own "calling," they should readily understand vocation's potential value to the identity—both secular and sacred—of their parishioners.

This issue is certainly worthy of our examination and of an honest response of self-examination. The focus of this chapter primarily has been that we who would dare to lead the people of God must always begin that journey at the center of our own being. The issue of money and stewardship is no different. In fact, if we take the words of Jesus with which we began this chapter seriously and personally, this is the primary issue about which we must ruthlessly examine our own hearts. Then, from true wisdom, humility and integrity, we can speak of spiritual principles to our fellow strugglers.

It now feels somewhat pedestrian to move to some of the practical issues that might strengthen the financial state of our congregations, yet it is probably what you hoped I would do all along …

When I arrived at the Cathedral of Hope in 1987 the church was on the verge of bankruptcy. It was unable to pay its bills or even the moving expenses of its own pastor. Though I took a 25 percent cut in pay, they still were occasionally unable to pay my full salary. With balloon notes coming due on the two buildings on their campus, they faced the distinct possibility of homelessness. The economy of Texas in the late 1980s neared depression levels with the collapse of the savings and loan, real estate, and oil and gas industries. Unemployment was high, and almost all of the significant donors in the church were bankrupt or dying. Even writing the description makes me wonder what on earth I was thinking by coming here.

With no endowments and few significant donors, 20 years after my arrival, our consolidated offerings reached $5 million, and we give away more than $1.3 million in services and assistance to the poor beyond our church. The social and economic circumstances today are substantially different, and we have many more members. What might be helpful is sharing some of the principles that contributed to that transformation, and some of the practical lessons I had to learn the hard way.

First, it was necessary to create an atmosphere of hope. No one invests in a sinking ship. If there is general sense that failure is inevitable then it is unreasonable to expect generosity. On the other hand, I have seen churches who had decided that they would ultimately close find a renewed sense of meaning and purpose in how they faced that final time faithfully. Having worked with many who were dying, most of us know that there often is a joy that goes far beyond the immediate circumstances. If that is not the work of our faith then what do we mean by resurrection?

In our case, hope began to break forth when we simply painted walls that had been water stained for too long. The next step was to remind a congregation that was literally dying of AIDS that it still had much to give. Turning inward and focusing on self-care had very nearly proven fatal. Mobilizing them to serve others in need was an instrument of rebirth. While many lesbian, gay, bisexual and transgender congregations were decimated by the AIDS crisis, ours experienced a genuine revival in every sense of that word.

Given the circumstances of the economy, and the staggering burden of our death rate and health crisis, it would have been easy to have slipped into a sense of scarcity. While I find the current "Prosperity Gospel" to be a clear violation of the most sacred teachings of Jesus, I do understand why it has found a hold in many minority or impoverished communities. When you are surrounded by, and confronted with, so many economic needs, it is easy to assume that there simply is not enough to go around.

That is not true. Today, more than any time in human history, we have enough. There is enough to eliminate hunger and poverty and much of the suffering they bring. The problem is not a scarcity of resources, but of will. Our job as spiritual leaders is clearly to convince our fellow disciples that we are responsible for helping our nation find the will. In some cases, it must begin by convincing our congregations that the resources are available for them to fulfill their vision.

In his book *Raising More Money*, Terry Axelrod tells a story of a friend who is a successful employee of Microsoft. His friend told an account of attending a fundraiser for an organization in which he deeply believed. Axelrod recounts his friend's story:

> *You know how much I love Organization X. They do incredible work internationally to end poverty and hunger. Their overhead is under two percent. Their total budget for the year, to do all they do, is only one million dollars.*
>
> *Last night was their annual fund-raising*

dinner here in Seattle. Their goal was to raise $100,000, or 10% of their whole budget. They succeeded. They were ecstatic.

I'm still upset about it ... that they were happy to settle for so little. I love that organization. If they had even thought to ask me, I'd have funded their whole budget for the year.

*Then I think to myself ... I'm sitting here right now on the Microsoft campus, looking out at all these people. So many of these people could have funded this organization several times over, of for that matter, funded **their** favorite charity many times over or fully funded that organization's endowment. But no one's asking us!*

Some years ago, when we announced our campaign to build a new facility, Pat Robertson's news program on the Christian Broadcasting Network (CBN) reported our intentions. They ended their report with a snide remark about the fact that, at the time, we did not have the money even to complete the architectural designs. That Sunday, as we launched our capital campaign, I showed a video clip of that taunt. Then turned to the congregation and said, "They are wrong about that. We **do** have the money to complete the design. We just haven't collected it yet, but we are going to change that right now." That morning, hundreds of people came forward and gave more than enough money to pay the architectural fees and to launch our capital campaign with which to begin construction.

However, giving a congregation a sense of hope that overcomes attitudes of fear and lack and scarcity is just the beginning. Ultimately, the leaders of the church must have the courage to actually ask people to give their money to our mission. This is all too often where we pastors fail. We never "close the sale." How often have we taught people the principles of living with generosity and gratitude only to watch them practice those principles with their alma mater, the local symphony or some other charity? The epistle of James rebukes us for that, saying, "You have not because you ask not." Sisters and brothers, "ask" is not a four-letter word. Millard Fuller, the founder and leader of Habitat for Humanity, likes to say, "I have tried raising money by asking for it and by not asking for it, and I always got more by asking for it."

While there are many ways to fund a church, almost all of them come down to asking people for money. As obvious as that may seem, it apparently is not so obvious to everyone. In a 1995 study 60 percent of Americans reported that they had been asked to give money; today fewer than 40 percent report that they have been asked by a church or nonprofit to give money. That decline means that millions of dollars simply was not given last year because no one asked for it.

Of all the money given away in this country 90 percent comes from individuals; 82 percent of that comes from families who earned $60,000 or less. Many churches and charities focus on the wealthy, but 78 percent of the under-asked say yes, which is six times as often as the wealthy say yes when asked. Of course, the wealthy get asked much more often, and they have ready their excuses for not giving. They are excuses, because those who make more than $250,000 a year give away less than 1 percent of their income, while those who earn less than $15,000 give 4 percent of their income.

So, while we could explore how you raise money from large donors, and there is certainly a science to that, ultimately, more than three-quarters of the money you raise will come from middle-class philanthropists. As good, progressive people, we have some guilt about the fact that those who can "least afford" to give away money will be funding our congregations. However, that attitude is really disrespectful to those who believe they have something to give. Most of them manage to feed themselves and their families and don't need us to give them free spiritual food any more they need the local café to give them free meals. Their self respect requires them to pay their way, and, to them, anything less would be theft.

In conclusion, let me list some of the very practical things we can do to help fund the ministry to which God has called us:

Have a Pledge Drive

I hate it; you hate it; they hate it. Still, it works. People who pledge give an average of three times more money than those who don't. If you decide not to ask for pledges then you have to spend more time fundraising in other ways, or reduce the amount of money you can raise. Perhaps a better strategy might be to reframe our annual campaign.

Like most churches, we used to do our stewardship campaign in the fall and connect it to the new year's budget. Then, one year, our calendar did not allow for that. Instead, we made it a part of our challenge to Lenten discipline. We asked people to try tithing (10 percent) for 40 days or, at the very least, to enter into a financial covenant as a part of their Lenten observance. This spiritual practice was coupled with a call to observe other classic disciplines of the church, as well as an "Experiment in Practicing Christianity." People were told that if they were faithful and the practices did not enrich their lives they could quit after Easter, no questions asked. Everyone was asked to sign a pledge of faithfulness.

We were staggered to find that, for the first time, the spring was our strongest season in every measurable way. Since that time, our congregation has come to practice Lent with great devotion. Today we call people in our membership classes to be "Covenant Keepers," and we give them a very nice pin to wear that symbolizes the six covenants they make at their confirmation to up hold the church with their prayers, presence, gifts, services, witness, and to continue to grow as a disciple of Jesus. Each Lent we try to find ways to remind our members of the covenant they made and to call them to renew those covenants **in writing**.

Rather than making the pledge drive a means by which to harangue people into underwriting the budget, why not find new and creative ways to incorporate it into a campaign to total spiritual renewal? Written pledges of prayer, service, devotion, generosity, etc. are all powerful. Why should we be more reluctant to ask people to sign a covenant than the local gym? We, too, are working to help people to be more disciplined and healthy.

Exploit the Shift from Giving to Spending

My parents give money to their church. They make a pledge every year, and every Sunday they take their check and they drop it in the plate when it passes. God love them, because they are a dying breed. There are fewer and fewer pure givers in America every day, yet charitable giving has actually increased most of the past decade. How can that be?

Many pastors that I talk to see news reports about the increase in charitable giving and shake their heads because that certainly has not been their personal experience. That is true with many charities as well. Most of the executive directors I know have to deal with budget short-falls. The breakdown seems to be that giving statistics are distorted because people have been responding generously to specific crises. Beginning with September 11, 2001, the American people have responded generously to disasters like tsunamis and hurricanes, but have not underwritten the operating costs of the churches and organizations that simply have sought to serve everyday needs.

The truth is that, when it comes to charities and churches, Americans are increasingly **spenders** not **givers**. Ask people to buy new hymnals or playground equipment and the money arrives in buckets, but the offering plate returns increasingly empty. Now, we have two options here. We can rail against this trend and try to hold back the tide, or we can figure out new ways to let this new reality fund the work of God.

Let me offer a couple of examples of how we have tried to ride this wave rather than resist it. We created a program called "Child of Hope" through which we serve children in need, including our own children and youth. Each year we receive a second offering during Advent and on Christmas Eve. We also give members the opportunity to give a donation to Child of Hope in honor of their family and friends rather than simply buying another gift that someone really doesn't need. If they will give us an address we send the recipient an acknowledgement card as their Christmas gift.

Through this program we raise thousands of dollars. The danger with programs like this, of course, is that we might divert money from the general fund to a designated fund that can only be used for the purpose for which it was solicited. To mitigate that we use an appropriate portion of the money raised to pay the salaries of the staff who actually manage the ministry and disperse the services. Through a wide variety of programs like this, we have raised more money and actually been able to lower our general fund budget without lowering services or reducing staff.

A few years ago, the Internal Revenue Service ruled that donations that are designated by the donor are not tax-deductible. Their explanation was that the donor was actually **spending** money not **giving** money. Donations are only tax-deductible if the institution is free to determine how the money is to be spent. Of course, money that our churches solicit for a specific purpose is tax deductible. However, if a donor simply decides to give money for a specific purpose because it was something they wanted, rather than something for which the church asked, then the donor is spending money not giving it. I have found this IRS ruling useful in helping donors understand the difference between spending and giving. Still, it is the cultural reality in which we must raise money today.

Increase Your Use of Technology

The Cathedral of Hope receives less and less money in the offering plate each year, yet our budget and income continues to grow. Every month the amount of money donated through our website increases. While we try to keep it discrete, we have asked our webmaster to ensure that on almost every page of the site someone has an opportunity to make a contribution should they choose to. In addition, nearly 25 percent of our donations are given automatically. By using a credit card or authorizing an automatic deduction from their checking account members contribute whether or not they attend. We have discovered that even people who move away often continue giving until they find a new church home.

Older members in long-established congregations attend church with great regularity. The average age of our congregation is almost 20 years younger than a typical mainline church. Because of that demographic, our people tend to attend much less often. Given the irregularity with which even our most dedicated members attend, the auto-

givers sustain the church in a critical way. By and large, the generation that has been acculturated to spend rather than give contribute only when present. For them, attending and giving once a month qualifies as active. Usually, when they sign up for auto-giving, it is at the rate at which they give when they attend. The net result is that their annual giving is substantially increased.

We also have placed a giving kiosk in the church where people who arrive at church without cash or checkbook can simply and quickly swipe their credit or debit card and make a contribution. For many years we have been told that we are moving to a cashless society. Today, that is true almost everywhere but the church. Even vending machines and parking meters have had to adapt to this reality. The more quickly the church does as well the better.

We use a service by which every member of the church is mailed giving envelopes monthly. The cost of this is much less than we would have to pay just for postage. We found doing so increased our giving by about 15 percent, and every person gets at least one mailing from the church every month. Recently, this company began mailing a series of cards to automatic givers that they can drop in the offering plate when it passes. This way it doesn't appear to their peers that they don't give.

Your Bible and Your Rolodex/Outlook

Every fundraising professional in your city will tell you that raising money is almost 100 percent about relationships. Frequently, leaders become renowned for the fact that they write notes to so many people. It is an amazing discipline if you will write two or three thank you notes a day. While emails are the modern equivalent, they still have not replaced the value of a handwritten note. Developing relationships with present and future donors is critical to the long-term financial health of any church or nonprofit.

When I came to the Cathedral we took Polaroid pictures of every person who attended membership class. I'd walk around for days with those pictures memorizing every name and any other information we might have. Even today I know the names of every one of the first 1,000 members. Then my RAM got full ... or something. Today I have a hard time remembering the names of my staff and board. While you may not have 1,000 people to get to know today, you should act as if you do, because if you remain in a community very long you soon will.

Before a fundraiser approaches a donor they learn absolutely everything they can about them. They want to know their giving history, what they like, who they are related to, how they vote, where they like to eat, what their pets' names are, and any other information that might possibly be helpful in getting the person to donate. How much more should that be true of pastors? None of our memories are sufficient. We must keep very good notes of phone calls and conversations.

We also need to collect every email and mailing address we possibly can. If you have ever tried to buy a mailing list to use you quickly discover just how valuable that information is to those raising money. Services such as Plaxo that are free and connect you to those who use the same system are also good. Most work through Microsoft Outlook and help you keep up with birthdays and can send "cards" to people on their special day.

In my own theological framework, the Bible is not the Word of God, but God often does speak to me through it. In those moments, it becomes God's word. So, too, record keeping is not a relationship and will not raise you any money, but diligence in this regard can enhance your relationships and become the source of funding.

Create an Effective Case Statement

Before launching any capital campaign a professional will ask the organization to create a case statement. That is probably a good exercise for anyone. While various people have definitions for what makes a good case statement, this is what I have in mind. In essence, it is a "data dump" that creates a central source for your mission, vision, passion, direction, strategy and unique philosophy. There is no need to state the obvious or to define the word "church." But this is a good place to state clearly how your church is unique, special, needed. You are making a case for your existence and funding. Why should I give you my hard-earned money?

In my opinion, the length really doesn't matter. It probably should be 15-30 pages long. You will never publish it or use it in its total form, but from it every piece of information about your church should be drawn. You should be able to hand it to a total stranger to create your website and s/he should be able to do so with complete accuracy based on your description of who you are and where you are headed. Although this document probably should begin with the pastor, it needs input from all the key leaders. It will be your unique bible from which everyone will draw their texts.

The document then needs to be boiled down into a two-page summary that all the leadership understands and integrates at a genetic level. It also needs a one-page version that every member can almost commit to memory. This version may become your welcome brochure or the document you give to potential donors who don't attend your church.

While there is much that could be written on this topic and others who are more qualified than I, let me offer some suggestions with regard to printed materials. Every document you produce should:

- Be customizable. Given the state of technology, there is no reason to give everyone the same information when people need very different information to motivate them.
- Use color. If you don't have the equipment with which to do this, there are businesses on every corner that can do it for you at a very reasonable cost. Select your colors carefully, though. Here a professional can be very helpful. You probably don't have to hire someone, since almost every company, institution or large business has someone who does this for them. Getting material designed may be a great way to get younger people involved in your ministry.
- Use an easily readable typeface. You are reading Palatino Linotype. Avoid Times New Roman and Courier. Use lots of "white space" to avoid overwhelming the reader.
- Use photographs. Carefully select them to elicit the emotional response you desire.
- Be proofed. Proof it, proof it again, and then have other people proof it. You will **not** catch your own mistakes. Presenting donors with material with a mistake communicates volumes and leads them to conclusions you'd rather avoid. You want to leave an impression of competency.
- Be edited. Edit it, edit it, and then have someone else edit it. Eliminate all extraneous words, phrases and descriptions. Boil it down to only the information you want to communicate. Remember white space is more likely to get people to read your information than your words are.
- Use headlines and subheadings effectively. That is all half the people will read unless you catch their attention.
- Never use abbreviations or insider language.

Denominations are notorious for using abbreviations so much that they forget what the initials actually stand for. The United Church of Christ frequently uses the initials OCWM. It stands for "Our Church's Wider Mission." Even the full title doesn't say anything except to true insiders. **Never** make a potential donor feel ignorant, uninformed or excluded.

I recently was asked to talk about the impact of a culture of fear on generosity. Certainly the events of 9/11, and the political leadership in its aftermath, had a devastating financial impact on many progressive churches. What I chose to talk about, though, was the impact of generosity on a culture of fear. This is the essence of our message. It is the point of our ministry. It is what we do and why we do it. Money is not a peripheral issue for our ministry, but, as Jesus said in the scripture we used at the start, our treasure is directly connected to our hearts, and to the hearts of those to whom we minister.

Chapter 12

What Was I Thinking?

by Rev. Dr. Jo Hudson, Senior Pastor, Cathedral of Hope

Late in 1993, during my last year of seminary, I became reacquainted with an old college friend. He invited me to dinner, and, during our conversation, I was stunned to learn that he had found a church home and was an active member. More than that, he was radiant with enthusiasm for his new church. He seemed to be a man truly transformed. In all the time I had known him during my undergraduate and graduate years in college, I had never known him to grace the doors of a church. Quite the contrary, he had been a playboy of sorts. Now, I sat across from a person who could talk of little else than the church he had found and the God who had found him.

Our reunion dinner contained one more bit of information. My friend shared with me that he was "gay." When I told him that I, too, was "gay," he insisted on setting up a lunch meeting with his pastor, Rev. Michael Piazza, then Senior Pastor of the Cathedral of Hope. I was well acquainted with the Cathedral of Hope. Few people in Dallas during the late 1990s missed the fact that the Cathedral of Hope was a large and fast-growing church with a primary ministry to, and with, lesbian, gay, bisexual and transgender people. It also was well known that this church, more than any other, had been a place of compassion and hope for hundreds who were living with, and dying of, AIDS. Still, the prospect of me, a deeply-closeted lesbian hoping for a successful ministry in the United Methodist Church—a church with church laws on their books that outlawed

LGBT people from ordained ministry—having lunch with the most "out" pastor in Christendom was daunting. It was my friend's passion and hope that convinced me to agree. Sitting before me was a man who was still very much the person I had known in college, yet within him was a light I had rarely seen in others.

Rev. Piazza and I met for lunch at a restaurant on Lemmon Avenue in Dallas, Texas. If there were others present, I cannot tell you any more than I can tell you the name of the restaurant or what we ate. I was deeply anxious, both because I was having lunch with a very visible "gay" pastor, and because I was having lunch with a pastor who was the leader of one of the largest churches in Dallas. What I discovered, as most people discover when they meet LGBT people, was a very "normal" man. He was interesting and funny; he spoke passionately and gently of the congregation he clearly loved; and he was respectful of me. It was clear to him, and to me, that I was not ready to make a dramatic shift in my ministry, and he graciously stated the obvious. We ended our lunch, and he made it clear that he thought that there might someday be a time when I would be ready. What I didn't know then was that his departing remarks to me were prophetic. He was calling me to a "higher place" of living fully as a human being and fully into the calling of being a minister of the Gospel.

Ten years later, in early January of 2004, after I had been "outed," left the United Methodist Church, and been graciously welcomed into the United Church of Christ, I found myself at the receiving end of an e-mail from Rev. Michael Piazza. During those ten years, our paths had crossed two, perhaps three times. I had responded to one of the Cathedral of Hope Daily Devotionals, and, within less than an hour, Rev. Piazza had responded back. He said that the church was in transition and that he did not have any women on the chancel. He asked if I might come to preach at the Cathedral of Hope. I was stunned, but what LGBT pastor wouldn't want an opportunity to preach at a flagship church like the Cathedral? So in April of 2004, I traveled to Dallas and preached for the first time at the Cathedral of Hope.

Just prior to my arrival, Rev. Piazza sent me an e-mail stating that the church had a job opening and he had some church leaders who would like to visit with me while I was in Dallas. I did not even take a breath before hitting the return button. I responded saying that I was not remotely interested, that I was happy in Bryan-College Station at Friends Congregational Church (UCC) and that my elderly parents were living there. I told him that I would visit with him and others, because I believed that you should always talk about opportunities, but that I simply wasn't interested.

The Sunday I preached in Dallas, Rev. Piazza made sure that I was part of the morning processional, and the rest is history. I was, in that moment, convicted by the Holy Spirit, the passion of the congregation, and the hope that filled the sanctuary. I told Rev. Piazza I would visit with him, and he and I began a conversation that would bring me to Dallas as a staff pastor with a long-term plan of moving into the role as Senior Pastor. All of this was contingent upon the relationship between the congregation and me.

What neither of us expected was that the transition would happen so fast. Within 10 months, the congregation was called together for the purpose of electing me as senior pastor of the Cathedral of Hope.

All of this is prelude to what I might offer from my experience and the experience of both Friends Congregational Church (UCC) in College Station, Texas and the Cathedral of Hope (UCC) in Dallas, Texas. I believe many pastors and congregations already know most of what I will share in the deep places of their hearts, but often do not attend to in their conscious minds because life and ministry take precedence over listening to God and discerning the movement of the Spirit.

Pastors and congregations perhaps should carve the well-worn idiom "expect the unexpected" over the entrances to their churches or, at the very least, the entrance to the pastor's study. Surely, as people of faith, we are those most equipped to understand that the Spirit of God will move where She will. Our challenge is that too often life and ministry take precedence over listening and discernment. As I look back at the transition I made to the Cathedral of Hope, I am certain that the Spirit of God was stirring not only in my life, but in the heart and soul of both congregations.

In the two years prior to being called to preach at the Cathedral of Hope, I had been restless. I had begun to read advertisements for pastoral positions in journals and on-line. I had taken a sabbatical in the hope that my energy would be restored. This is not to say that I wasn't happy in my ministry at Friends Church. I was extremely happy, loved the people of the church, and continued to pray that God's Spirit would guide and enliven us that we would be faithful disciples of Jesus, but I was tired. My prayer became, "Oh God, if I need to go or you need someone else here, show me the way." So, why was I surprised when two years later an opportunity presented itself?

Similarly, when I interviewed with the people of Friends Congregational Church I had said that it was my hope to be there in ministry for seven to 10 years. I was in my seventh year of ministry when I was called to the Cathedral of Hope. More importantly, if the leadership of the church and I had been paying attention, we would have noticed that, in that year, the church was at its strongest. We had finally crested the 300-member mark, we were worshiping in three worship services each week, and, more than all of that, we had seasoned leaders taking responsibility for ministry and encouraging and empowering others for that ministry. Had I a chance to do it over again, I would have called our leadership to prayer, would have invited them into a season of discernment, would have been aware of the stirring of the Spirit both in me and in the congregation. Instead, we did what most congregations do: we pushed ahead.

It is my sense that most individuals and churches actually can "expect the unexpected" if they will tune their hearts to God's song. We might better have anticipated the change had I shared my exhaustion and restlessness with the leadership of the church and I had helped the leadership realize that the growth and strength of the church might be a preparation for change. I am relatively clear that we both let fear regulate our relationship rather than trust in the Spirit of God among us. I was afraid to admit my weaknesses. The church was afraid that I would leave. Instead of being afraid, we might have been honest, but it is my experience that honesty is best born out of making a place for God. Neither the church nor I were able to do that, but, as the elected pastor of the church, it was my responsibility to guide the leadership and the congregation in that process. In that respect, I failed.

Still, I am happy to say that Friends Church was as ready for the change as I was. The congregation rallied at the announcement of my departure. They cared for me and celebrated my ministry, and we parted amidst laughter and tears. I think it is fair to say that the congregation struggled with the transition, as do all congregations, but the strength of faith amidst the people saw it through a time of transition, an interim ministry and, ultimately, the call of a new pastor. I learned recently that in 2007, on the Sunday of the annual Christmas pageant, there literally was only one empty chair in the entire building. The congregation is now making plans for a capital campaign to expand its overflowing facilities. Yes, it is safe to say that Friends Church, filled with the Holy

Spirit, in expecting the unexpected, has thrived as a part of the Body of Christ in College Station, Texas.

The journey of my ministry and the transitions within the Cathedral of Hope are equally joyful, but not without the unexpected. When I arrived at the Cathedral, I was aware that the church was in transition. The congregation had weathered an attack on the senior pastor, a withdrawal from its denomination, the departure of all of the pastoral staff, save Rev. Piazza, the Senior Pastor. I knew all of this, yet the depth of the struggle could not be fully known until it was experienced. My encouragement to pastors taking new positions is to learn as much as you can about the current circumstances of your new calling, but be prepared for the fact that you cannot, and will not, know all you need to know until you are immersed in the life of the congregation.

My own experience proved, yet again, that I could expect the unexpected. I don't seek to be trite or to take lightly the circumstances into which any pastor steps, but I think it is safe to say that things are always worse than the leadership of the congregation, pastors and staff say they are. However, I find that the opposite is also the case: No matter how good you think things are, you can expect that they will be even more so. A congregation that has faced its demons and named its weaknesses, clung to God and sought the Spirit, and tried its best to be the face of Christ is one that knows the truth that Paul wrote in his letter to the church at Rome:

> *Not only so, but we also rejoice in our sufferings, because we know that suffering produces perseverance; perseverance, character; and character, hope. And hope does not disappoint us, because God has poured love into our hearts by the Holy Spirit, whom God has given us.*
>
> Romans 5:3-5

A congregation that has lived this truth is one that will not only survive but thrive and create unexpected and profound joy.

There are more unexpected moments in the transition from a 300-member congregation to a 4,000-member congregation than I can count, but among them is that as much as things are different they are the same. The move to a large congregation means that there are some differences in the way you do ministry. In my first year of ministry, and even now, Rev. Piazza said to me, "You can't do that. You need to delegate that to someone else." Clearly, the move to a larger congregation with a staff means that the personal, day-to-day contact with the congregation changes. The ability to have working knowledge of all parts of the church changes, but the principles of ministry do not. The Senior Pastor of a large congregation must give attention to the macro issues of the church: vision, worship, budget, human resources. The direct ministry needs to be toward the staff and key leadership of the church, though I believe it remains important to have a weekly contact with the people in the pews through teaching, occasional attendance at key gatherings and some personal pastoral counseling. The key to it all is finding a balance between administration and ministry, being present, and one's personal care.

The unexpected part of it all came when someone, in my first year at the Cathedral, asked if the change from my previous church to the Cathedral of Hope had been a radical change. While I was asked that frequently in my first year, I finally took some time to contemplate it. My answer is simply this: The truth is ministry is ministry. You never have enough people to do all that you believe God is asking of you. You never have enough money to do all the things you believe God is calling you to do. You have proportionally the same numbers of people: 20 percent of the people sustain the life of the church through their gifts and ministry, while 80 percent of the people take far more than they give. You have proportionally the same numbers of people who have high social or physical needs, and people who are mean-spirited, but you also have proportionally the same number of people who are saints. And the roof leaks. I've never served a church where the roof didn't leak. All of that is the same whether you have a membership of 100, 300 or 4,000.

Having experienced ministry within both a small membership church setting and ministry in a large membership church, I would say that, while there are many things that probably are vastly different, two stand out. The first has to do with stress. While I thought that I was deeply stressed during ministry at Friends Congregational Church (UCC) in College Station, the stress I have experienced as Senior Pastor at the Cathedral of Hope-UCC is very different. At Friends Church I worried about what I would call "close range" issues: Will the person who said that they would provide communion actually show up? Is there enough coffee for the fellowship time? Did we get the parental approval for each youth participating in the mission trip? Do we have a pianist for Sunday? Has someone proofed the worship guide? A case in point was that for several years our congregation sang the refrain of a hymn entitled "Ours the Journey" as our benediction response. I remember that at one point the worship guide had a typographical error that read, "God of rainbows, fiery pillows." Well, of course, it should have read, "God of rainbows, fiery pillars." It took weeks before we finally got the template to the worship guide changed and the correction made. It was frustrating and, in some ways, embarrassing that it took so long to correct. This is the minutiae that can consume and eat away at the soul of a pastor.

Still, "God is good and God's steadfast love endures forever." (Psalm 100:5) As perhaps only a small, closely knit faith community can do, the "fiery pillow" typo became fodder for many jokes and, at the service that ended my ministry at Friends, "the fiery pillow" once again made an appearance in a gift made to me by the congregation.

In contrast, the stress of a large-member church is the burden of being responsible for so much. It is estimated that most congregations expect their pastors to be experts in approximately 16 different areas of ministry to include: preaching, teaching, pastoral care and counseling, leadership development, volunteer cultivation, financial management, fundraising, youth work, worship leadership and liturgy, grief counseling, and building maintenance. The list goes on. While all pastors labor under these challenges, the pastor of a large church has the added pressure of all of those responsibilities as well as a working knowledge of human resources and staff development. While the pastor of a large-member church has a staff to help offset the minutiae of ministry, ultimately, all paths lead to the door of the senior pastor. Now, instead of worrying if there will be enough money to pay your salary each month, you have the additional worry of whether or not there will be enough money to pay the salaries of many other people. I believe that many pastors who take on a large membership churches are rarely prepared for the kinds of responsibilities and conversations in which they find themselves.

For example, I recently mentioned to one of our staff members that, in my wildest dreams of ministry, I never thought I would spend time talking about a five million dollar capital campaign and soil borings. Nothing in seminary prepared me for that possibility.

Of course, the management of this kind of stress can be mitigated by a regular prayer and devotional life, by acknowledging that you don't know nearly enough, and by surrounding yourself with people who know more about specific areas of ministry than you do. None of this was information I knew when I arrived at the Cathedral of Hope, but have learned over the course of time in this amazing church and through the support and guidance of my predecessor, Rev. Piazza. He and I both have had the chance to say to one another, "If you are not currently scared out of your wits, then you don't have a full grasp of the situation." Of course, some of the most common words in scripture are, "Do not be afraid." I cling to that truth.

The second issue I have found to be significantly different between a small-membership and large-membership church is that conservative evangelical churches are the most predominant and visible in the arena of large-member, or mega-, churches. Consequently, they are viewed as the model. Since coming to the Cathedral of Hope, I have been struck by the sometimes subtle and sometimes blatant bias against large-member churches. I attended a preaching conference, and, in the questions to the speakers and in their responses, there was a clear negative bias against large-member churches. There seems to be a dislike and distrust of churches that have harnessed the amazing gifts of technology. There also seems to be a belief that large-member churches are only interested in numbers, both in people and money. I think there also is a general assumption that large churches have all the people, money and resources they need. I can say all of this because I was among those who held those beliefs at one time. However, being at the Cathedral of Hope has opened my eyes to a different reality.

Although I cannot speak for all large churches, I can say that my experience at the Cathedral of Hope has taught me that all churches, regardless of their size, have the same goals: to bring people close to God, to help them grow in faith, to help them love their neighbor, and to help them in their journey to be faithful disciples of Jesus Christ transformed by the Holy Spirit, loving God with heart, mind, soul and strength. I hope that is our common goal and desire. Large-member churches are able to do some things that small-member churches cannot do: host key speakers and preachers, workshops, youth programs, etc. Similarly, small-member churches can create an intimacy of community that large member churches have to work very hard to create and maintain. Small-member churches can keep up with their congregation far better than larger churches.

I recently heard a member of a small church say, "We love each other. We check on each other. We do things together. We go places together, sometimes spontaneously." And I thought to myself, "We do that." The difference is that we have to work to create those smaller communities within our larger church setting instead of having it built in.

While I realize that many people have a bias against large-member churches, it is always my hope that grace abounds and that we ultimately see that God is a God of immense creativity and diversity and, in that, has called into being all kinds of churches to be co-creators with God in bringing God's realm to reality on earth.

Ultimately, I believe that the size of the church has little impact on the vitality and sustainability of a church. I also believe that style of worship is not the issue. If we are going to be churches that are vitally alive—not just sustaining the life of the church but growing the spiritual life of those who come, empowering them to be active disciples of Jesus who impact their communities and world—there are a few things that I believe have to happen.

At the point the pastoral leadership of the church changes, I believe it is incumbent upon the incoming pastor to embrace the vision of the church as it exists unless, of course, the vision and ministry of the church is toxic. If the church is relatively healthy, the incumbent pastor need not wipe away all that her or his predecessor has done. Rather, trust that the congregation has an inherent knowledge of its history and has made a commitment to its vision and then step into the vision and help sustain it.

When I arrived at the Cathedral of Hope, the church had an impressive history, as well as a well-defined vision statement. It was in the midst of a long-term capital development plan that would create a chapel and cathedral designed by world-renowned architect Philip Johnson. I knew immediately that, even if I personally was not ready to build a chapel or cathedral, that the congregation was and had invested greatly in this vision. I chose to work with Rev. Piazza and the existing staff to continue to articulate that vision.

Equally, I believe it is important for the new pastor to begin to formulate their own way of speaking the vision to the congregation. It is important for that pastor to trust their insights, discernments and gifts and to know that they can take what has gone before them, reframe it in language that they are comfortable with, and still maintain the direction of the vision.

I believe this is what has happened at the Cathedral of Hope. Gradually, as I got my "land legs" and began to know the history and vision of the church, I was able to frame the challenges to the congregation in language, and ministry, that was comfortable to me, while still honoring the work of my predecessor and the vision of the church. As we went through pastoral change, both Rev. Piazza and I told each other and leaders in our congregation how much we wanted this transition to work and how we were both committed to the long-term vitality of this congregation, and that we believe that some of its best years were still ahead of it.

I believe that any congregation, at any stage in its life and history, can choose to be a prophetic church constantly in renewal. In fact, as I believe Rev. Piazza has already stated, if a church wants not just to survive but thrive then it will constantly seek to re-invent itself according to what the church believes God is asking of it, by following carefully the teachings of Jesus, and by being open to the direction of the Holy Spirit. This is not easy but essential.

Finally, I believe that any congregation can restore its vitality by making a commitment to radical hospitality, passionate worship (regardless of what style of worship is used), excellence in preaching, the commitment to caring for others beyond its walls—feeding the hungry, caring for the poor, etc.—and the willingness to tell others about your faith.

Ultimately, however, you can expect that, in the midst of all of that, all that God really wants is your heart. If you give your heart to God then you can expect that the Holy Spirit will show up and will blow through your church like a mighty wind and will change all of your plans. You likely will find yourself saying, "What was I thinking?" When that happens, rejoice for the unexpected is likely to happen, and nothing in your life will ever be the same again.